Being a Christian Educator

Discovering Your
Identity, Heritage, and Vision

Being a Christian Educator

Discovering Your
Identity, Heritage, and Vision

William B. Rogers

Smyth & Helwys Publishing, Inc.
Macon, Georgia

ISBN 1-57312-092-8

Being a Christian Educator
Discovering Your Identity, Heritage, and Vision

William B. Rogers

Copyright © 1996

Smyth & Helwys Publishing, Inc.
6316 Peake Road
Macon, Georgia 31210-3960
1-800-747-3016

Library of Congress Cataloging-in-Publication

Rogers, William B. (William Benjamin), 1938–
    Being a Christian educator:
    discovering your identity, heritage, and vision/
    William B. Rogers
    x + 102 pp.   5.5 x 8.5 (14 x 21.5 cm.)
    FaithGrowth: 1
    Includes bibliographical references.
    ISBN 1-57312-092-8 (alk. paper)
    1. Christian education—Philosophy.
    I. Title. II. Series.
    BV1464.R62   1996
    268'.01—dc20   96-38533
                                                CIP

Contents

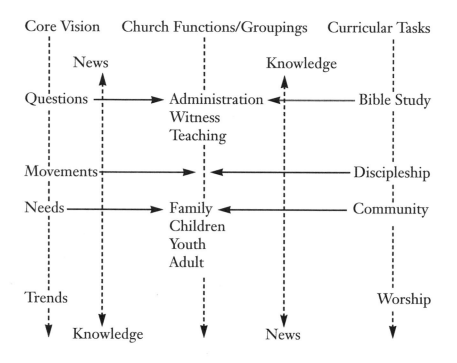

Core Vision   Church Functions/Groupings   Curricular Tasks

              News   Knowledge

Questions ──────▶ Administration ◀────────── Bible Study
                  Witness
                  Teaching

Movements ──────────▶   ◀────────── Discipleship

Needs ──────────▶ Family ◀────────── Community
                  Children
                  Youth
                  Adult

Trends   Worship

        Knowledge   News

Synergism of Contents

Core Vision

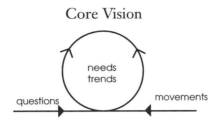

questions   needs trends   movements

Curricular Tasks

Church Functions/Groupings

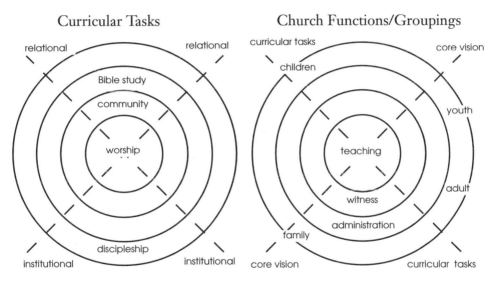

Knowledge/News

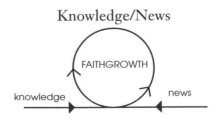

knowledge   FAITHGROWTH   news

To those who bring the
chemistry and alchemy to life

Luwilda McKaig
Jason Benjamin
Melissa Alexandra

Preface

While engaged in the preparation of this manuscript, through the writing of Ian Bradley, I was introduced to "the Celtic way" in a formal manner. Celtic Christianity flourished in the British Isles from approximately 400 to 1000 A.D. The Celtic artwork, sculpted crosses, lyrical prayers, classical hymns, and illuminated manuscripts represent a spiritual renaissance in a period known otherwise as the Dark Ages. Bradley comments:

> Celtic Christianity does seem to speak with almost uncanny relevance to many of the concerns of our present age. It was environment friendly, embracing positive attitudes to . . . the goodness of God's creation. It was nonhierarchial and nonsexist . . . it takes us back to our roots and seems to speak with a primitive innocence and directness which has much appeal in our tired and cynical world.[1]

The Celtic way places a high premium on three concepts: presence, poetry, and pilgrimage. Presence refers to the immanence of God, the interconnectedness and interdependency of everything that is then understood to be linked to God. Poetry is seeing beneath the surface of things and expressing what is recognized and discerned. Pilgrimage is the exploration that goes on throughout life, the end of which is to arrive where we started, knowing the place for the first time.[2]

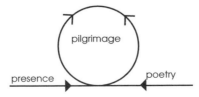

Celtic Christian art has a theme of constant movement. This dynamic is found in the "endlessly intertwining movements of the Celtic knot"; it is revealed in the "swirling curves and spiral of the illuminated manuscripts."[3] The lines travel onward even as they double back on themselves, crossing over each other and ultimately coming back to where they started.

The Celtic story is one of oppression, suffering, and marginalization; but it is also a story of hope, imagination, and wholeness. "What is primitive and simple can also be profound and original. Among the voices of the most marginalized and oppressed we may find the greatest wisdom."[4]

I have learned that the Celts found the presence of God mediated in daily routines and in ritual and ceremony. "Getting up, kindling the fire, going to work, going to bed were occasions for recognizing the presence of God."[5] One obvious lesson we can learn from them is reinvestment of the ordinary with a measure of sanctity. Ritual and ceremony were thought to invest a measure of transcendence in birth, marriage, and death events.

Again and again in Celtic Christianity the purpose is "not to explain . . . the mysteries of faith or open them up on a dissecting table, but to suggest and marvel at their infinite depth and subtleties."[6] It is my cherished hope that this "vision of Christian education" will be received without the expectation that it should "explain mysteries," but rather with the expectation that it should engage in a dialogue that suggests and marvels at the "infinite depth and subtleties" of Christian nurture.

William B. Rogers
England/Scotland, 1995

Notes

[1]Ian Bradley, *The Celtic Way* (London: Darton, Longman, and Todd, 1993) vii.

[2]Ibid., 83.

[3]Ibid., 2.

[4]Ibid., 30.

[5]Ibid., 39.

[6]Ibid., 98.

Identity, Heritage, Vision

Contents

We are living in an age that has moved to include non-linear thinking with linear. We are warned to prepare ourselves for paradigm shifts. We are exhorted to "get it" with the "information age" as the "third wave." I propose that Christian education move to a new way of thinking that will shift the paradigms of educational ministry. The evolving "Table of Contents" is used to demonstrate how the new thinking might create new paradigms.

The "traditional table" demonstrates linear thought, proper indentation, separation of categories, and a logical sequence of thought. In the second table "nontraditional" language is used for labeling. The traditional outline form is abandoned, linear thought continues in modified form, and a different type of logic operates. Notice that the third version of "contents" is not even referred to as a table. In its place an unusual word appears: *synergism*. Synergism suggests a quality of interaction, organic flow, and a connectedness. Horizontal and vertical lines that characterize both the traditional and nontraditional tables are rare. Circular lines and interactive arrows now dominate.

Synergism is related to the biological term *synergy*—"the working together of two or more muscles or organs." The Greek word *synergos*, from which "synergy" is derived, means "working together." This understanding was foundational to the development of the theological term synergism. Historically, that doctrine attempted to bring together the activity of divine grace with human activity, working cooperatively to produce regeneration.[1] We have "the combined action of two or more activities which have a greater total effect than the sum of their individual effects." The form of the word that means "to work with, cooperate" is *synergetic*. *Synergistic* means producing or capable of producing synergy.

I find it necessary to shift our images of Christian education away from mechanistic images to organic images. The dictionary definitions assist us in moving toward that paradigm shift. In this vision statement, I am searching for the synergistic model in Christian education that is capable of producing the synergy of faith growth.

An alternate title for this series might be "Encountering Christian Eucation Again, for the First Time!" In a sense, what I propose here isn't new at all. This approach to Christian education is an attempt to recapture that which is foundational, engaging, and energizing.

Core Vision

This volume is an attempt to clarify visions for Christian education. Some Christian educators have published such works that offer a satisfying degree of integration and internal coherence. Their integration is illustrated by an insistence that biblical and theological themes must bleed through all chapters. Other attempts, however, have been characterized by an unfortunate fragmentation and internal dissonance. Their fragmentation is illustrated by volumes with early chapters concentrating on biblical and theological themes that are then ignored in subsequent chapters. Integration and internal coherence are the goals of this present attempt to state a vision for Christian education.

Theological, biblical, and philosophical issues beg attention and reflection. It is inadequate, however, to give attention with authoritarian finality. Therefore, these issues are examined here in the form of "questions of faith conviction." The emphasis is on faith growth. The convictions are not static but dynamic. They are timeless and relevant. They are certain and elusive.

Too often it is accurate to describe our culture as one with little awareness of our history and heritage. It is also accurate to describe many of us in the contemporary church as persons with little awareness of the heritage and history of the Christian church. We are like a newly hatched chick pecking mindlessly at the shell fragments that have nurtured us and given life. In this attempt at clarification, historical movements will be identified by the phrase, "movements of educational ministry." Faith growth is not all bud and blossom; it has root systems also.

In the classical sense of Christian education, the examination of the biblical, theological, philosophical, and historical bases represents a comprehensive treatment of a vision. But more recent times have taught us that the needs of persons and groups are of equal significance in the vision. Yet, we have learned also that a fixation on contemporary environments can mislead us. We can focus attention in Christian education on groups and individuals to the neglect of the formative influences over the preceding centuries. The "needs of contemporary persons" and the "trends of contemporary environments" will translate the language of psychology, sociology, and other social sciences. Faith growth is intended to be a comprehensive and inclusive term indicating a proper consideration of both the classical concerns and the more recent concerns.

Curricular Tasks

Often one inadequacy in the practice of Christian education is its pursuit of a superficial understanding of curriculum. Is the curricular task limited to theological propositions and its interpretive materials (as illustrated by a catechetical approach)? Is the curricular task expansive to the degree that it includes all of life's experiences in the totality of living (as illustrated by an existentialist approach)? Is the task located properly somewhere between these two extremes?

To be more adequate, the curricular task must be understood organically, not mechanistically. I propose that it is best located in a synergistic center influenced by both the institutional needs of the organization and the relational needs of persons (see Synergism of Contents). Therefore, the four curricular tasks are not programs primarily, but constant needs that demand attention by the Christian educator. Relational needs are vital in the curricular task lest a mechanistic understanding dominate the task allowing the corporate ego needs of institutional pride to overwhelm the needs of persons in relationships. Conversely, a preoccupation with individual needs of selfish pride can block sensitivities to the needs of a healthy covenant community.

Several questions are suggested to address the curricular tasks. How much of our ongoing ministry of Christian education is designed to respond to the unique needs of the individual? How much responds to the stereotypical needs of individuals? How much addresses an inordinate preoccupation with institutional self-centeredness?

Faith growth develops in that synergistic seedbed where Bible study, discipleship, community, and worship are informed by both relational and institutional influences and expectations.

Church Functions/Groupings

A first function assigned to Christian education is administration. A misappropriation occurs, however, if administration becomes the consuming activity of the Christian educator. Yet, that function is indispensable in the covenant community. Administrative functions should be evaluated to determine their relationship to core vision and curricular tasks.

A second function appropriately assigned to Christian education is the witness of the church. The witnessing community embodies its own purpose and primary identity in evangelism and social action. Too often the witness through social action is neglected.

The third function is teaching. The teaching ministry of the church has been understood erratically in the various expressions of Christian education. Christian nurture should be offered to both inquirers and believers. This function would be enriched if more Christian educators thought of themselves as teachers in the functional dimensions of Christian education.

Stages, phases, and categories dominate our understanding of the chapters of life. They will facilitate our study and reflection on the groupings in the life of the church. Each of these four group-ings will receive priority treatment in a separate volume of this series: Family, Children, Youth, Adult.

Knowledge\News

Let me tell you a story. Two women are riding on public trans-portation one spring morning. Each is following a routine to leave home and go to work in an office building located in the city. A family pattern has preceded the departure from each woman's home. Early morning habits with children and husband have been observed. The route to work is predictable with no detours. Upon arrival at her work station, each woman begins a ritual of work habits that consume the day. At the conclusion of the workday, each returns home to the duties and patterns that characterize life in the suburbs.

One woman encounters the usual and uneasy silence of the morning routine in the presence of her husband. Animated con-versation disappeared from their communication long ago. This couple has surrendered their once cherished hopes about redeco-rating their home and about establishing a college fund for their children. Both hopes faded in the alienation between them. The children fail to join them for breakfast. The morning meal has been displaced by a different menu for each family member. Conversation has been supplanted by sound and pictures coming from three different TV sets. The ride to work affords a mind-numbing parenthesis that offers twenty minutes in which this woman can deny the indifference with which she approaches her work. It is a job that was intended to pursue an economic advan-tage for her family. But now, she is trapped in the job that has become an economic life jacket for the family's survival. At the end of the day, she will return home to the domestic chaos. After fulfilling multiple responsibilities, with no sense of them being shared, she will fall into merciful sleep sometime after midnight.

The other woman and her husband have disciplined them-selves to a 5:00 A.M. alarm three mornings each week to grant the two of them a three-mile walk through their neighborhood and intimate conversation over a cup of coffee before the children arise. Each parent has divided the domestic workload and, with uneven success but continuing good humor, delegated responsibilities to each child. As she rides to work, the second woman notices the spontaneous beauty of spring. She reflects on the headlines of the morning that indicate places where war and hunger will block any joyful celebration of spring this year. While it is true that her job has a mindlessness about it, she makes an effort to know her co-workers. Today, she wonders how to speak to one of them about a death in that co-worker's family. She anticipates the domestic chores of the evening, but she relishes the fact that this is the one evening each week when each parent will take one child and devote the entire evening to that child. Whether it is a basketball game or a homework assignment, it always serves to strengthen the bond between the children and their parents.

What may we say about the two women in this story? One is not awake to life, relationships, world events, or her environment. The second woman has made some modest but intentional effort to wake up to life, relationships, events, and environments. Both women have knowledge available to them, but the second woman knows some of the same knowledge as news. The knowledge has affected her condition.

Tabloid journalism has devalued and trivialized the word *news* in our environment. As the word is used in this material, news is understood as "making known the information about important facts and considered perspectives which have a bearing on my condition."

Here is the difference between a piece of knowledge and a piece of news: Knowledge can be arrived at by anyone, anywhere, anytime. News, on the other hand, is not available anywhere, at anytime, to anyone, because it is uniquely relevant to the situation of the person encountering the information. Knowledge becomes news when it is drawn from the context of living. The person who hears the news is the person who encounters a situation. News is precisely the communication that has a bearing on my condition.

In judging the significance of a piece of news, everything depends on the condition of the person. If a person lives in a cave and hears the cry "Come—this way out," the communication qualifies as news if that person is longing for an exit. If another person has come to the cave to spend the rest of his life, the announcement will be of little significance. It will be only knowledge. To a person dying of thirst, information about the sale of VCRs is insignificant. But information about water is important "news."

The trustworthiness of the person bearing news is also significant. If the person bearing the knowledge is my sister, if I know that she knows my predicament and she comes to me with the appearance of genuine concern, if the knowledge relates to my condition, then I hear the knowledge as news. Walker Percy writes:

> If one thinks of the Christian gospel primarily as a communication between a newsbearer and a hearer of news, one realizes that the news is often not heeded because it is not delivered soberly. Instead of being delivered soberly . . . it is spoken . . . and calculated to stimulate emotions. But emotional stimuli are not news.[2]

Emotions can be stimulated anytime, anywhere, by any person. This is only one illustration of the struggle facing Christian educators. Each of us could provide illustrations of emotional stimuli parading as news.

So in Christian education what we seek is not knowledge, but news. What we hope for is not static information, but dynamic news. What is desired is not a disjointed listing of content, but the news that is engaged with our condition. What we need is the pulse of life, an interactivity, an organic flow, a connectedness.

Our search for a vision is unfulfilled by propositional faith handed to us by external sources. We search for a vision that finds meaning with questions of faith conviction and movements of historical antecedents as they interact with needs and trends. The curricular task is not satisfied by programs as isolated components, but finds satisfaction in holistic systems that face up to needed ecclesial reforms.

While we as Christians must be awake to life, relationships, events, and environments, as Christian educators we must be the agents to awaken others to life in the body of Christ. That is another way of expressing the good news that is in Christ Jesus.

Finally, this volume will address knowledge and news in Christian education as it is fed by paired influences. The development of Christian instruction imposed from an external authority will be engaged with the reactionary development of Christian nurture derived from the expression of the internal self. These competing ideas will be called to the synergism of the knowledge and news of faith growth. This synergism leads us to ask: Where is the locus of authority? What is the source of authority? Where are religious authorities located?

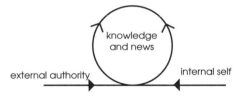

Procedurally derived discipline and free, spontaneous activity will be pulled to a synergistic center characterized by disciplined activity. We are led to ask: What is liberating discipline? How do procedural discipline and free activity come together?

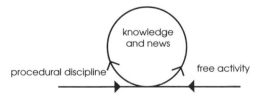

Faith growth derived from texts and teachers, and faith growth derived from immediate experience will be integrated with a synergy of the contemporary experience and historical experience. We then ask: What are we to learn from experience? How are we to blend the contemporary and the historical?

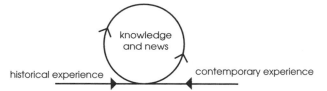

Faith growth based on static claims and materials will be brought into dialogue with the changing world. Where the changeless truth and the changing world listen to each other, knowledge and news are realized. The questions emerge: Is there a still point to the turning world? Is there a synergistic center?

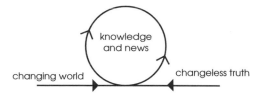

In summary, I intend to state a vision for Christian education that calls for the synergism of the knowledge of a core vision, the knowledge of curricular tasks, and the knowledge of functions and groupings that will yield to the possibility of becoming news. I pose the question about the locus of authority and suggest that the synergism of the knowledge of the internal self and the external authority must be open to become news. The question of discipline is proposed as something to transform into liberating discipline. Historical experiences and contemporary experiences must be poised to become synergistic news related to one's condition. Finally, the synergy of the changeless truth and the changing world interact to become good news, the gospel.

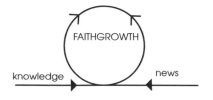

Notes

[1] *The New Lexicon Webster's Encyclopedic Dictionary* (New York: Lexicon Pubs. Inc., 1990) 1003.

[2] Walker Percy, *The Message in the Bottle* (New York: Farrar, Straus and Giroux, 1975) 135.

Core Vision

W̶hile I was attending a conference for theological educators in the mid 1980s, one participant interrupted the discussion with this question: "Do we all agree that God was in Christ Jesus?" The inquiry was prompted in the mind of that individual by earlier statements of several other participants. The question was elemental. It elicited responses that offered clarity. It facilitated subsequent discussions. Although we did not agree on every issue related to theological education, we did subscribe to that vision of the incarnate Christ. Not every participant chose identical language to elaborate that formula in the stated question. That Christological vision, though, has become a core faith conviction for that group of theological educators in the context of a continuing dialogue over the past decade.

The following questions are deceptively simple to describe, but their answers are devastatingly costly to embody!

Questions of Faith Conviction

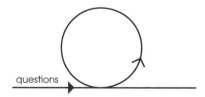

Individual:
What is my identity as a child of God?

Educator:
What is our identity as God's people? How recently has that understanding been affirmed, adapted, or revised in this congregation?

Who Am I?

Who am I? They often tell me
I stepped from my cell's confinement
Calmly, cheerfully, firmly,
Like a squire from his country-house.
Who am I? They often tell me
I used to speak to my warders
Freely and friendly and clearly,
As though it were mine to command.
Who am I? They also tell me
I bore the days of misfortune
Equably, smilingly, proudly,
Like one accustomed to win.

Am I then really all that which other men tell of?
Or am I only what I myself know of myself?
Restless and longing and sick, like a bird in a cage,
Struggling for breath, as though hands were compressing my throat,
Yearning for colours, for flowers, for the voices of birds,
Thirsting for words of kindness, for neighborliness,
Tossing in expectation of great events,
Powerlessly trembling for friends at an infinite distance,
Weary and empty at praying, at thinking, at making,
Faint, and ready to say farewell to it all?

Who am I? This or the other?
Am I one person today and tomorrow another?
Am I both at once? A hypocrite before others,
And before myself a contemptibly woebegone weakling?
Or is something within me still like a beaten army,
Fleeing in disorder from victory already achieved?

Who am I? They mock me, these lonely questions of mine.
Whoever I am, Thou knowest, O God, I am Thine![1]

The phrase "child of God" usually refers to those who have entered into a trusting relationship with God. Such persons have acknowledged God as the source of their life. All persons are created by God, they bear the image of God, and they should be respected in light of those convictions about their relationship to God. Not everyone has an unbroken knowledge of and communion with God, but God wants a parent/child relationship with each of us. The Bible has a variety of metaphors to describe the process by which we become a "child of God" (adopted, begotten, born anew—John 3; 1 Pet 1, 2). It is in and through Christ that we are adopted, begotten, or reborn to become God's people.[2] My identity as a "child of God" begins here. Our identity as "God's people" continues here.

Christian education has a vital concern to enable persons to discover their identity as children of God. Even more, our task calls us to answer the question about our identity as God's people. It is a perennial assignment in Christian education to lead congregations in affirming, adapting, or revising that understanding of corporate identity.

As congregations move through stages of life together in Christ, periods of corporate history will demand the affirmation of identity as it has been subscribed to in the past. Other stages and periods of the church's history will dictate a revision and adaptation of statements regarding the congregation's identity. For example, in the early 1990s, a congregation in Louisville, Kentucky, decided to adopt a phrase affirming their Baptist heritage. They recorded it on the permanent sign posted on the busy street on which their church building is located. Directly under the name of the church, the phrase of identity affirmation now reads: "Committed to historic baptist freedoms."

As persons move through stages of faith in Christ, certain characteristics can be noted. Walker Percy describes it like this:

> A person who looks at a group picture looks for himself first: everyone else in the picture looks more or less as he knew they would—they are what they are; but he does not know what he is, and so he looks to see; and when he finds himself, he always experiences a slight pang. So, that is who I am![3]

A spiritual version of these tendencies is observable when we search for our personal identity as a child of God. We are curious about our identity as Christians in comparison with those believers around us and, vicariously, with believers presented to us in history and story. Often much more information is available to me about your religious identity, and much less is available to me about my own religious identity. So it is in Christian congregations that we are afforded the opportunity to satisfy more of our spiritual curiosity. In Christian community, my own spiritual identification becomes more available, more accurately through others in that communion.

Individual:
How do I find forgiveness and hope?

Educator:
How do we as a congregation express forgiveness and hope?

What is the difference between expressing an apology and expressing forgiveness? The United States government apologized to Japanese Americans for placing them in relocation camps, but did not apologize to American Indians for killing most of them. The U.S. House of Representatives and the U.S. Senate approved formal apologies to native Hawaiians for the overthrow of Queen Liliuokalani engineered by the United States government 100 years ago. Japan apologized for its treatment of Koreans during World War II. An Austrian official apologized in 1991 for his country's support of the Nazis. Even the Vatican apologized for its judgment of Galileo. The judgment was delivered in the seventeenth century; the apology was issued in the twentieth century. An apology expresses regret. It may also be a formal acknowledgement or excuse.

In 1990, the Alliance of Baptists confessed complicity with racism and in repentance asked forgiveness of African Americans and God. In 1992, the Cooperative Baptist Fellowship offered a similar statement. The Baptist Peace Fellowship of North America sponsored a comparable statement in 1993 entitled "The Birmingham Confession." Confession and repentance are pivotal words and concepts in forgiveness. Forgiveness is an act of God's grace to forget forever and not hold people of faith accountable for sins they confess. On the human level, forgiveness is the gracious human act of not holding wrong acts against a person.[4]

> Then Peter came and said to him, "Lord, if another member of the church sins against me, how often should I forgive? As many as seven times?" Jesus said to him, "Not seven times, but, I tell you, seventy-seven times.
>
> "For this reason the kingdom of heaven may be compared to a king who wished to settle accounts with his slaves. When he began reckoning, one who owed him ten thousand talents was brought to him; and, as he could not pay, his lord ordered him to be sold together with his wife and children and all his possessions, and payment to be made. So the slave fell on his knees before him saying, 'Have patience with me, and I will pay you everything.' And out of pity for him, the lord of that slave released him and forgave him the debt. But that same slave, as he went out, came upon one of his fellow slaves who owed him a hundred denarii; and seizing him by the throat, he said, 'Pay what you owe.' Then his fellow slave fell down and pleaded with him, 'Have patience with me, and I will pay you.' But he refused; then he went and threw him into prison until he would pay the debt. When his fellow slaves saw what had happened, they were greatly distressed, and they went and reported to their lord all that had taken place. Then his lord summoned him and said to him, 'You wicked slave! I forgave you all that debt because you pleaded with me. Should you not have had mercy on your fellow slave, as I had mercy on you?' " (Matt 18:21-33)

As Christians, we are commissioned to embody repentance and confession and forgiveness in the name of Christ. The core vision for Christian education includes an acknowledgement of the thirst for forgiveness that exists in some measure in the life of every person. But the vision expands toward embodiment in our corporate presence as the body of Christ. As Christian educators, we have the obligation to apply this concept both individually and collectively. Within our ecclesiastic subculture, we apply the transaction of forgiveness more adequately on the level of the individual than on the level of the collective. The illustration of the confession with racial complicity is a positive example of the collective application.

The second half of the proposed questions seeks to find and express hope.

> Martha said to Jesus, "Lord, if you had been here, my brother would not have died. But even now I know that God will give you whatever you ask of him." Jesus said to her, "Your brother will rise again." Martha said to him, "I know that he will rise again in the resurrection on the last day." Jesus said to her, "I am the resurrection and the life. Those who believe in me, even though they die, will live, and everyone who lives and believes in me will never die. Do you believe this?" She said to him, "Yes, Lord, I believe that you are the Messiah, the Son of God, the one coming into the world." (John 11:21-27)

Charles Poole wrote about our connection with these words:

> We look an awful lot like those two sisters today. We have experienced what they experienced. We have felt what they felt. We have either said what they said, or we have wanted to and did not do it. We have felt the hard blows of the twists and turns of life. We have stood by the open grave. We have sponged at the raging fever. We have sat by the all night bed. We have waited on the all-day surgery. We have heard our parents breath to the rhythmic beeps and blinks of intensive care artillery. We have been stunned by the biopsy. We have been stung by the criticism. We have stood with the sisters where the ground shifts beneath our feet and life turns out differently from the way we had it planned. . . . Jesus hurt with Mary and Martha. Jesus walked with Mary and Martha. Jesus wept with Mary and Martha. And then, despite the fact that the sisters' faith was all mingled with anger, regret, and disappointment, Jesus gave the sisters more than they hoped. Jesus raised Lazarus from his grave to live a little while longer.
>
> And then, later, God raised Jesus from his grave to live forever. This is the ground of our hope. The resurrection tells us that this is God's world. The resurrection tells us that, while the worst things can and do happen, the worst thing that happens is never, never, never the last thing that happens. The resurrection is our last and only reason to whisper hope.[5]

Hope is not the only word we know. Hope is just the last word. From the perspective of the Creator, the Redeemer, and the Sustainer, it appears that the last word is hope. We are commissioned to be persons of hope. As Christian educators, we are lashed to a vision of hope. It is crucial to our vision of the church. Where is hope? It is in the vision for God's people. Where is hope? It resides with Christ in the Christian community.

Individual:
Where do I learn to practice accountability in community?

Educator:
How do we embody mature forms of accountability in the covenant community?

Unlike the question regarding identity, or the question regarding forgiveness and hope, the third question of faith conviction is not recognized universally. Not everyone knowingly acknowledges a thirst for accountability on a perennial basis. Throughout the history of the Christian tradition, however, believers have expressed various degrees of engagement with the practice of accountability within Christian relationships.

While serving a church, one of my fellow ministers resigned his position and left the church and his family under scandalous circumstances. Among the ministers who were left on the church staff, we found ourselves being praised and coddled for our fidelity to the church family and our own families. Every group, except one, wanted to celebrate my virtues. That one group had become soul mates to me in my Christian pilgrimage. They knew me better than any other group. Together we had committed ourselves to mutual accountability before God, with clearly stated disciplines for our life together. While they cared for me and my family in the turmoil engulfing our congregation, they also said to me, "Bill, we think your self-righteousness is becoming insufferable as you are compared to the minister who departed. We want to ask you to revisit the story of the prodigal son, with emphasis on the son who stayed home!" I will always cherish the mature form of accountability exercised in our covenant community.

Monastic orders represent the more extreme illustrations of these engagements. Several functions were characteristic of those orders. An individual functioned as a "prior" or moderator or shepherd in the order. For a group to learn to practice accountability in mature forms, some person must serve the group as shepherd. Intercessory prayer for each group member is an obligation of the shepherd. Employment of the spiritual gifts of each group member is a function fulfilled by the shepherd. The Christian community with mature forms of accountability will need the presence of a shepherd or prior.

Another contribution of the monastic tradition is found in the function and title "spiritual director." This person enhances accountability by selecting structures of study for each individual and the group. While these structures are selected collaboratively, the director is given authority by the group and the individual to hold them accountable. To illustrate, structures refer to the minimum disciplines such as participation and obligations for study and ministry.

A third function in the formula for accountability is that of "pastor-prophet." It is vital that one individual in the group serve as both pastor and prophet. Each of us has an appetite for the presence of those who encourage, support, and nurture us—which are appropriate pastoral qualities. Accountability in the covenant community also requires the presence of those who confront, challenge, and demand of us—which are appropriate prophetic qualities. Both of these qualities need to be expressed by one person who is gifted with compassion, but who never surrenders the gift of confrontation.[6]

Minimum disciplines are required if mature accountability is to be achieved. They must be stated with simplicity and clarity before a group member declares membership. Minimum disciplines are *not* goals or objectives; minimum disciplines are serious commitments to be struggled with on a daily basis. What are examples of minimum disciplines?

Prayer	*Bible Study*
Worship	*Community*
Giving	

Is any Christian opposed to these five as goals? I doubt it! Is any Christian opposed to these five as disciplines? Why?

We are not surprised by the description of these disciplines, and we acknowledge their validity; but few of us have known structures of accountability in which these minimum disciplines were incorporated. This is a vision statement for Christian education.

We are not discussing the unfettered access to salvation in Jesus Christ. Instead, the surface issue of access to church membership and Christian group membership is discussed. We know from experience that "successful churches" (given our sports and business mentality, statistically advancing churches) with sophisticated and elaborate plans and organization can be stimulating. Churches with exciting worship experiences may have some immediate energizing value. Rarely do these same churches make serious commitments to the reconciling work of God in Christ. They become ends in themselves. They demand more people to sustain their plans and experiences. Too often, these churches are reduced to inviting persons to enter sensational and limited experiences rather than a new life of discipline and sustained accountability.

Many religious groups enlist persons to belong faithfully, but sustained accountability is missing. I am confronted with an impossible task when I have not found what I am attempting to help others find: a mature form of discipline in the covenant community.

Individual:
How do I sense direction through the spirit of God?

Educator:
How do we practice mutual affirmations of the direction we discover through the spirit of God?

"They are more baptistic than we Southern Baptists are baptistic." Those admiring words were spoken by a Southern Baptist leader. The time was the mid 1970s, and the congregation that was the object of admiration was Church of the Savior in Washington, D.C.

One of two prime factors of discovering a sense of direction among Christians in Church of the Savior is the concept and practice of journey inward/journey outward.[7] This concept is supported not only in written and oral expressions of the congregation, but also in the practical requirements of mission groups and their minimum disciplines.

The journey inward is a commitment to the development of prayer and study. It emphasizes the interior life of the pietistic tradition in the Christian's spirituality. The journey outward is a commitment to the servant life of mission and ministry. It emphasizes the external life of the social witness tradition in the Christian's spirituality.

Have you known persons who were consumed with the journey inward? Have you lived through chapters of your life devoted to prayer and study? Did that commitment to the pietistic tradition consume the available energies of your life?

Have you known persons who were consumed with the journey outward? Have you lived through chapters of your life devoted to mission and ministry? Did that commitment to the social witness tradition consume the available energies of your life?

How are we to strike a balance? How are we to help others find equilibrium between the journey inward/journey outward? How are we to sense direction through the spirit of God? How are we to be fortified internally while maintaining sensitivities externally? How are we to form a Christian spirituality that engages both the devotional life and the servant life? How are we to fashion more than a rhetorical commitment to internal and external dimensions of spirituality? As Christian educators, how are we to provide structural and relational commitments to this concept? The answers to these questions will give us a sense of direction through the spirit of God. They will enable us to practice mutual affirmations of the direction we discover through the spirit of God.

The second prime factor points to needs and gifts. How are they discovered? Primarily, God uses two clues. One clue is found in the needs of the world in which you live. The other clue is found in the individual gifts with which God has endowed you to enable you to be who you were meant to be and meet some of those needs.

(1) Find what God is doing in the world, and join in that work. Matthew 25 is a good starting point. In verses 31-46, we are instructed to join God in feeding the hungry; providing drink for the thirsty; and offering hospitality to the stranger, clothing for the naked, visitation to those who are sick, and a presence to the imprisoned. Evidently, God is concerned about technical work to grow more food more efficiently; projects to provide friendship and love for lonely persons; medical research to cure diseases; human rights for the oppressed; efforts to realize peace on earth; and strategies in institutions, governments, businesses, and churches that demonstrate a primary concern for persons.

(2) Each of us is empowered as a Christian with a gift that we are to use in serving others. Ephesians 4:4-13, 1 Corinthians 12, and Romans 12:3-8 refer to these special gifts. These gifts carry us into the world. Through them we pursue avenues of self-discovery and liberation. Our obedience and practice of our gifts allow us to find a sense of direction through the spirit of God. When we find this sense of direction and affirm that discovery in others, we are becoming more like God.

When are Christians most like God? When engaging in ecclesiastical activities? No, God is involved with us in our best worship and study, but God is equally involved with sweeping events of our world that have their impact on all of God's children. When are Christians most like God? Christians are most like God when they do what must be done in relationship to God, family, vocation, and friends. Christians are most like God when they engage in the giving of their gift in the name of Christ. Christians are most like God when they do what they can do uniquely in the context of life that has been granted to them.

Be warned though, that sense of direction through the spirit of God for which we have so desperately yearned, we may already have and know. We do not possess and do not have access to pure, transparent reason and inspiration. All that comes to us is mediated by a variety of influences. What we need, we cannot earn. It is a gift from God offered graciously. Truth will not be found in what is delivered or invented by agents of manipulation. Recognizing those agents is enormously difficult. At times, consequences will defy the best of intentions. Rarely is there a straight line from design to result, from cause to effect. The one we name God is greater than our understanding. We must be reverent in our expression of theological ideas.

Individual:
How do I engage with others as followers of Jesus and relate to the structures of institutional power in my world?

Educator:
How do we nurture the body of Christ and respond to the forces of institutional power that threaten the church?

One of my central observations as a Christian educator is the uniqueness of our assignment in ministry to monitor the forces of institutional power. We have the obligation to assure the fidelity of Christian programs and structures to Christian convictions.

All organizations and institutions live with the continuous threat of becoming unfaithful to their mission. Monitoring that fidelity is an activity that never ceases in its appropriateness. Structures and programs are not value free. For example, what messages are communicated when visitors arrive at our church building for Sunday School? In the stereotypical transaction, what values are conveyed when we determine the visitor's proper placement in Sunday School by asking for the person's age or grade? Could we make a more informed, sensitive placement of the person if our questions determined the answers to these or similar questions: "How long have you been a Christian?" "Are you familiar with our denominational tradition?" "From this menu of placements, which Sunday School class descriptions are of more interest to you?"

In the past, we have used the stereotypical questions because they are more efficient. The organization is more productive if we use questions that are less time-consuming and more superficial. When we worship at the feet of the gods of efficiency, we are threatened by the forces and structures of institutional power.[8]

The nature of power is illustrated in the account of the temptations of Jesus as it is found in the Gospels of Luke and Matthew. It is one of the most important stories in all of literature. Through the Grand Inquisitor, Dostoyevsky asks if it were possible to imagine that the three temptations Jesus confronted in the wilderness at the beginning of his ministry were lost to us:

> had they perished entirely from the books and if we had to restore them; If we were required to invent them anew, would it be possible to do so? If we gathered all the persons of wisdom, the rulers, the chief priests, the philosophers, the poets and gave them the task of expressing three questions such as would fit the occasion: that is, express in three phrases the whole future history of the world and the human experience, Could they in their wisdom create anything which has the depth and force equal to those three phrases put to Jesus?
>
> For in these three questions, the whole subsequent history of the human race is, as it were, brought together into one whole and foretold, and in them are united all the unsolved historical contradictions of human nature . . . nothing can be added to them or taken from them.[9]

Each temptation wears a mask of benevolent power. It is power to meet material needs, power to control political institutions, power to use God for good purposes. In his *Inferno*, Dante places an obscure thirteenth-century pope, named Celestine V, at the very center because of what Dante calls "his great refusal" or his resignation from the papal throne after only five months. Ignazio Sillone, an Italian writer, treats Celestine V more sympathetically, attributing his abandonment of the papal throne to the realization on his part that the desire for power to do good is the most dangerous of all human desires. As he explains to some of his old friends:

Power is a difficult horse to lead: it goes where it must go, or
rather it goes where it can go or where it's natural for it to go. . .
. The ambition to command, the obsession with power is, on all
levels, a form of madness. It devours the soul, overwhelms it,
makes it false. Even if you aspire to power "to good ends" especially if you aspire to power "to good ends." The temptation of
power must be the most diabolical that can be held out to a person, if Satan dared propose it even to Christ.[10]

While visiting with a friend who is the dean of a university, I
questioned the rationale behind the policy that allows a faculty
member to serve as dean for a five-year period only. His unflinch-
ing answer was, "We have discovered that to remain in a position
of dominance for more than five years allows that person to gather
a destructive amount of efficiency and power!"

The physicists have known power, and this is a knowledge
they cannot lose. In the heady days of discovery regarding the
splitting of the atom, Robert Oppenheimer said, "When you see
something that is technically sweet, you go ahead and do it, and
you argue about it only after you have had your technical success."[11] The search for releasing the power of the atom continued
at Princeton and Los Alamos. The search reached a plateau in the
desert of New Mexico in 1945 at a site named "Trinity." In the
disillusionment and despair of the late 1940s, Oppenheimer
looked back on the first detonation of an atomic weapon and the
cosmic power unleashed there and wrote:

> We knew the world would never be the same.
> A few people laughed,
> A few people cried,
> Most of us were silent.
> I remembered the lines from Hindu scripture:
> Now I am become death,
> I am destroyer of worlds.[12]

We must be careful not to repudiate power. Power is necessary in our world. Our society operates from bases of power, the
power of individuals to make decisions, to change the course of

events, the power of groups to influence policy. Power is not sinful in and of itself, but it can become sinful. The worst sin is when it masks itself as power to do good. Karl Rahner wrote, "It can demonstrate better than anything else what is the true nature of sin: the desire to be like God"[13]

The "no" to service, the installation of self-will, the substitution of the finite for the absolute, power for power's sake—which is a sin . . . When power for power's sake is hidden behind a mask of benevolence, the final betrayal of good takes place. Because each of us has unique gifts and God-like affinities, we are tempted to arrogance. We can overstep our strength and become unauthentic. Within the boundary of our intended purpose, we have powers on which we are called to exercise in ways that no animal or atomic particle is called to exercise.

Reflecting on the evils of the Nazi regime, Thomas Merton was moved to describe his own appetites for power. Later, looking back on world events, he wrote:

> That I should have been born in 1915, that I should be the contemporary of Auschwitz, Hiroshima, Vietnam and the riots in Watts are things about which I was not first consulted. Yet they are all events.[14]

There is no fixed solution to the power dilemma. We may not avoid the question "what will we do with our power?" There is no "living happily ever after" in relation to power. The dilemma of what to do with it is something we begin to face as we move out of infancy, and it remains with us through every stage of life's pilgrimage.

So here we are—back to where it all started. The struggle with the decision in the desert is one we face every day. We do not all have the same amount or forms of power, but each of us has within our control some energy that can make things happen. The question is, what do we do with that power? The alternatives are arrogance and apathy—the temptation either to do too much or too little. There is no evading the problem. It will be with us every minute of our lives. The Christian educator has a unique responsibility related to structures of institutional power.

Guidelines

I will use four biblical images as guides for reflecting on movements in educational ministry. Not only is the content of these
passages instructive, but their context is illuminating.

> Hear, O Israel: The Lord is our God, the Lord alone. You shall
> love the Lord your God with all your heart, and with all your
> soul, and with all your might. Keep these words that I am com-
> manding you today in your heart. Recite them to your children
> and talk about them when you are at home and when you are
> away, when you lie down and when you rise. Bind them as a sign
> on your hand, fix them as an emblem on your forehead, and
> write them on the doorposts of your house and on your gates.
> (Deut 6:4-9)

This passage is given the classical designation "Hear Thou," or
"Shema." It became the highest confession of Judaism, "Hear, O
Israel." Rabbinic law establisheD the ancient ritual of reciting the
Shema morning and evening. Rabbinic tradition reports that the
Shema originally contained only verse 4, but was later to include
verses 5-9.[15] When Jesus was confronted with the question about
which law was supremely important, he answered with the Shema
(Matt 22:34-40; Mark 12:28-34). The content calls for loving God
and loving others with our total being. The context for reciting
these words is within the fabric of living. Neither the content nor
the context acknowledges limitations. This provides our first
guideline:

**Educational ministry is judged in any age by this radical and
comprehensive call.**

> When the Son of Man comes in his glory, and all the angels
> with him, then he will sit on the throne of his glory. All the
> nations will be gathered before him, and he will separate people
> one from another as a shepherd separates the sheep from the
> goats, and he will put the sheep at his right hand, and the goats
> at the left. Then the king will say to those at his right hand,

"Come, you that are blessed by my Father, inherit the kingdom prepared for you from the foundation of the world; for I was hungry and you gave me food, I was thirsty and you gave me something to drink, I was a stranger and you welcomed me, I was naked and you gave me clothing, I was sick and you took care of me, I was in prison and you visited me." . . . Then they also will answer, "Lord, when was it that we saw you hungry or thirsty or a stranger or naked or sick or in prison, and did not take care of you?" Then he will answer them, "Truly I tell you, just as you did not do it to one of the least of these, you did not do it to me." And these will go away into eternal punishment, but the righteous into eternal life. (Matt 25:31-36, 44-46)

Matthew 25:31-46 is the exam that will be presented to all persons and nations. There is no hint of a question in theology or how we articulate theology. The emphasis is upon the quality of our ministry. Our true relationship with Christ is reflected in how we compassionately respond to other human beings, especially where there is hunger, sickness, or imprisonment. This does not mean that we are saved by our good works. It means that if there is a trusting relationship between us and Christ, something of his existence rubs off on us, and we come to embody some of the qualities of his way of life. This presents us with a second guideline:

Educational ministry is judged in any age by mission acts of compassion offered in the name of Christ.

Now on that same day two of them were going to a village called Emmaus, about seven miles from Jerusalem, and talking with each other about all these things that had happened. While they were talking and discussing, Jesus himself came near and went with them, but their eyes were kept from recognizing him. And he said to them, "What are you discussing with each other while you walk along?" They stood still, looking sad. Then one of them, whose name was Cleopas, answered him, "Are you the only stranger in Jerusalem who does not know the things that have taken place there in these days?" He asked them, "What things?" They replied, "The things about Jesus of Nazareth, who was a prophet mighty in deed and word before God and all the people, and how our chief priests and leaders handed him over to be condemned to death and crucified him. . . . Then beginning with Moses and all the prophets, he interpreted to them the things about himself in all the scriptures.

As they came near the village to which they were going, he walked ahead as if he were going on. But they urged him strongly, saying, "Stay with us, because it is almost evening and the day is now nearly over." So he went in to stay with them. When he was at the table with them, he took bread, blessed and broke it, and gave it to them. Then their eyes were opened, and they recognized him; and he vanished from their sight. They said to each other, "Were not our hearts burning within us while he was talking to us on the road, while he was opening the scriptures to us?" (Luke 24:13-20, 27-32)

This is the exhilarating and humbling story of Jesus as profound teacher and the disciples as confused, stumbling learners. In *Christian Religious Education*, Thomas Groome reflects on this passage and what it tells about Jesus the teacher:

He begins by encountering and entering into dialogue with the two travellers. Rather than telling them what he knows, he first has them tell . . . what their hopes had been. . . . He recalls a larger story of which their story is a part and a broader vision beyond what theirs had been . . . he continues to wait for them to come to their own knowing. He spends more time in their company. . . . Eventually, in their table fellowship, they "came to see." Thereupon, they set out immediately to bear witness to what they now knew.[16]

The dialogue between the situation of the biblical story and the individual's own story provides us with a third guideline:

Educational ministry is judged in any age by the presence of a dialogic principle coupled with a faithful witness to the Christian story.

So Peter invited them in and gave them lodging.

The next day he got up and went with them, and some of the believers from Joppa accompanied him. The following day they came to Caesarea. Cornelius was expecting them and had called together his relatives and close friends. On Peter's arrival Cornelius met him, and falling at his feet, worshiped him. But Peter made him get up, saying, "Stand up; I am only a mortal." And as he talked with him, he went in and found that many had assembled; and he said to them, "You yourselves know that it is unlawful for a Jew to associate with or to visit a Gentile; but God has shown me that I should not call anyone profane or unclean. . . .

Then Peter began to speak to them: "I truly understand that God shows no partiality, but in every nation anyone who fears him and does what is right is acceptable to him. You know the message he sent to the people of Israel, preaching peace by Jesus Christ—he is Lord of all." (Acts 10:23-28, 34-36)

Acts 10:1-48 is the powerful story of the apostle Peter and his discovery of the narrowness of his vision of the gospel. He learned the elemental facts about the universal meaning of Christ that he had failed to grasp in the company of Christians in Jerusalem. Finally, Peter was able to see that God shows no partiality. The walls of exclusivism always fall under the truth of God's grace. In many chapters of the educational ministry of the church this experience has been replicated. Conversation within the fellowship of believers can blind us. We are handicapped by the provincialisms of our own pronouncements. Experiences outside religious circles make us aware of our Christian mission. This leads us to a fourth guideline: Educational ministry is judged in any age by the startling challenge to wake up.

In summary, to reflect on movements of educational ministry, these questions are the guidelines:

• Is there a radical and comprehensive call to love God?
• Are persons engaged in mission acts of compassion in the name of Christ?

• Are persons nurtured through dialogue and witness to the Christian story?
• Are persons challenged to wake up to the presence of the spirit of God?

Movements of Educational Ministry

Movements in educational ministry may be broken into three periods: the Early Christian Movement (Jesus–600 A.D.), the Reformed Christian Movement (1400–1700), and the Sunday

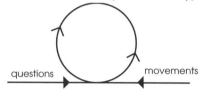

School Christian Movement (1700–1900). In this section each movement will be presented, and the guidelines that have been identified from the four biblical images will be used for reflection. For more than twenty years, I have used the outline of learner, teacher, curricular/method for organizational purposes when examining historical movements of educational ministry. I will use that pattern in this section.

The Early Christian Movement

The early Christian movement begins with the public ministry of Jesus. Think about the New Testament stories you know and the persons who were learners gathered around Jesus. They were representative of diverse racial and ethnic backgrounds. Economic and social differences also characterized the disciples in the early Christian movement. Social, vocational, and gender boundaries were torn down in the early circle of believers.[17]

In this apostolic period of church history, families were responsible for nurturing children as learners. It is reasonable to assume the existence of some form of intergenerational study defining each participant as a learner whatever the age of the person. Given the importance of families in this movement, it is easy to see why the house church concept is rooted in this period.

Reflection Using Guidelines. Since our four guidelines have their genesis in this formative period of Christian movements, it is reasonable to affirm their presence at this time. By the end of this era, in the fifth and sixth centuries, a radically different picture of the learner had emerged. Now there are categories of learners who must enter and depart from worship based on their status. Some are classified as "hearers" because they are considering the Christian faith. Others are being instructed for baptism, while yet another group of learners is engaged in penitential acts. One group of learners has even achieved the superior classification of "the faithful!"[18]

It is understandable that these developments should occur from an educational point of view. Yet, the turmoil these developments foster must be acknowledged. Here we have the seeds of institutionalism.[19] Institutionalism is always a threat to the church. These classifications begin to create dissension among learners. They suggest both superior and inferior levels of learning. But, more significantly, these structures of prejudice begin to move away from radical and comprehensive calls to love God. The busyness with securing status misses the demand for acts of compassion. The Christian story is lost in a preoccupation with the individual's story. The learner tends to go into a spiritual stupor rather than waking up to the spirit of God.

From the events of the crucifixion, resurrection, and ascension of Jesus until approximately 600 A.D., the teachers warrant identification. Clearly, the apostles were given a commission to teach because they had been with the historical Christ. The oral tradition of ethical living (the Way of Life and the Way of Death)[20] served a teaching function; the confessions of faith were also an elemental piece of the oral tradition of the apostolic church.[21] The creeds were used by teachers in the oral tradition. According to W. A. Quanbeck,

Oral instruction was necessary; few Christians could read. . . .
Yet maintaining an oral tradition in the faith instilled a certain
life . . . the message lived in the heart.[22]

Tertullian of Carthage (born 160 A.D.) and Origen (born 185
A.D.) were teachers of great significance in the early Christian
movement. Tertullian favored a radical break between Christians
and non-Christians. He was extremely suspicious of the Greek
and Roman culture of his day. Origen, on the other hand, under-
scored the importance of Greco-Roman learning. He began his
lecture by pointing to the similarities between philosophical and
theological thought. He was well respected by non-Christian
teachers.[23]

In the early Christian community, the curriculum was accessi-
ble to few in written form. For the sake of clarity, I need to inform
you that the prevailing understanding of curriculum will shift
from one historical context to another. In this period, the written
content of the curriculum included:

• The "Tradition" or the Gospel
• Letters from Paul
• Manuals for church officers (for example, 1 and 2 Timothy)
• Sermons (for example, Hebrews)
• Apocalypses and visions (for example, Revelation)[24]

The curriculum was shaped by difficult questions that needed
discussion in the company of the committed:

• How do I handle personal possessions?
• How do I handle social rank?
• How do I divide tasks?
• Do I mix with nonbelievers?
• How do I order family life?[25]

In the centuries following Christ's earthly ministry, the
curriculum of the Western church gave attention to scripture,
fasts and vigils, rites, and reading apostolic letters. The evolving

hierarchy of the church had a profound impact on the curriculum of the church by the fifth century as well.

Over these centuries, three types of gatherings demonstrate the methodology of the early Christian movement:

• Christian meetings of the Word that included various types of prayer, psalms, hymns, spiritual songs, reading from apostolic letters, reading from the *Didache*, and words of prophecy.
• Christian meetings for the common meal and communion that included those in the fellowship (Acts 2; 1 Cor 11)
• Christian meetings to attend to the business of the group (1 Cor 6; 2 Cor 2)

Reflection Using Guidelines. In reflecting upon our guidelines and this first movement of educational ministry, the radical and comprehensive call to love God is diluted as the formality of church structure displaces the spontaneity of the apostolic story. The demands to serve the institutional church can supplant the command to serve others in the name of Christ. Church histori ans remind us that the leaders of the church attempted to bring all of human society under the authoritarian control of the church by the sixth century in many regions of the Mediterranean world. The Christian story must be rediscovered in every movement.

The Reformed Christian Movement

Calvinism played a significant role in the theological thought of the Reformation. Although the Reformation was broader than the Genevan movement, for the purpose of this vision statement, the Reformed church under Calvin is a helpful case study. Max Weber's analysis of this case study is enormously revealing. In contrast to pre-Reformation Catholicism, Calvinism provided a religious rationale for charging into the world, remaking the world, methodically reshaping the world, and planning the routines of daily life. Labor was no longer a curse but an opportunity to work for divine glory.[26]

Who were the learners in the Genevan church as ordered by John Calvin? Learners were to be found in each of the four columns that supported the structure of the Calvinist theocracy. Those four columns were church, home, school, and state.

The church provided the ultimate goals of education for the schools and the ministry of the Word and sacraments. The school nurtured students to become qualified ministers, teachers, and lay leaders. The school qualified learners to become Christian administrators and citizens. The home gave birth to the persons who would be fashioned for those ordained purposes in the state and the church. The state served that godly kingdom. The four columns worked together to form an effective theocratic system of education. Whatever posture a Christian educator assumes toward Calvinist theology, this theocratic system is a marvelous piece of machinery to behold.

In this system, the teachers were to be found in the church, the school, and the home. Parents, ministers, and schoolteachers were qualified in catechetical instruction. They were given authority to speak decisively for God. This system identified the role of the teacher authoritatively in the church as a separate function from that of the pastor.[27]

This systematic approach to Christian education used Christian doctrine in propositional forms to provide the content of the curriculum. The content translated into a catechetical methodology. The theocratic machinery was implemented with overt demands and procedures of discipline. Unapologetically, elders were given the primary task of enforcing the machinery of discipline. Pastors were required to meet periodically for the express purpose of giving mutual criticism of each pastor's faults.

Reflection Using Guidelines. What shall we conclude about our guidelines and the Reformed Christian Movement as it was established in Geneva? The call to love God was comprehensive. A theocratic approach to the Swiss city-state satisfies that guideline. Furthermore, the Reformation was a radical movement.

Reflecting upon our second guideline in the Genevan church raises several questions. Why are attitudes that result from judgments to disperse religious doubts and give certainty of grace expressed with so little compassion? When faith is proven by objective results, who should be surprised by an environment of efficiency in method and meanness of spirit?

Efficiency and productivity are rarely compatible with the pace and rhythm of dialogue. Dialogic understanding requires a complex and mysterious process that does not lend itself to propositional statements delivered with the authority of the catechetical instructor. If success and expansion in the world are viewed as success in the eyes of God, then the religious movement is on a collision course with biblical views of success. Waking up to the spirit of God is not the equivalent of waking up to the principles of capitalist expansion.

The Sunday School Christian Movement

The Sunday School movement contained developments in educational ministry from 1700 to 1900 in England and North America. Initially, in England, the learners were children of lower class families who were taught by the adults from upper class families. Educational efforts to teach reading skills have never met with universal approval! Upper class fears were mixed with upper class benevolence in England in the early development of the Sunday School. In most denominational traditions, the Sunday School has assumed that the children are the learners. By the late 1800s, the children were graded with the vocabulary of beginners (birth–5 years), primaries (6–8 years), and juniors (9–12 years). When the twentieth century arrived, teacher and parent education programs and strategies had defined adults as learners as well.

The teachers were selected to work in the Sunday School based on their religious and charitable motives. This was a lay-led movement outside the established church. When Sunday School Societies were developed in North America, the class system was dissolved by the cherished ideal of the democratic principle. Teachers were selected on the basis of their missionary zeal. In the westward movement of the Sunday School from the eastern seaboard to the upper Ohio River valley, Sunday School "Union Missionaries" were appointed.

In the early nineteenth century, the curriculum was limited and primitive. The methods were drill, memory, and recitation. The Uniform Lesson series was launched in 1872. That literature component of the curriculum took on impressive qualities of organization and relevancy in the first two decades of its publication. Issues of racism, liberal theology, the social gospel, and progressive education were pursued in the curriculum of the Sunday School before 1900.[28]

Reflection Using Guidelines. In the developments of the Sunday School in its first two hundred years was there evidence of a radical and comprehensive call to love God? Not precisely. There was a lay-led call to express benevolence and build loyalty to a volunteer organization that advanced Christian ideals and cultural values. But were the acts of compassion in the name of Christ observable? In multiplied instances such acts were observable. If not always offered in the name of Christ, at least they were offered in the name of Christian civility. If they were not that, then they were offered in the name of missionary motives to "Christianize America so America could Christianize the world."

Did the Sunday School movement offer to nurture through dialogue and witness to tell the Christian story? In isolated illustrations it did, but that dialogue and witness easily was lost to the need for multiplying organizations and building loyalty to the organization. The rise of a capitalist economy; a democratic political system; a populist, progressive education; and an independent church tradition were converging streams that produced a cultural river and a cultural story that overwhelmed the Christian story in many instances.

Was there evidence of a challenge to wake up to the spirit of God? Timid challenges did occur. There are more illustrations of those who stayed with a small vision of the gospel. Limiting contacts and communication within the fellowship of the Sunday School movement continued to create blind spots and other spiritual handicaps.

The early Christian movement, the reformed Christian movement, and the Sunday School Christian movement are representative of educational ministry that must interact with the questions of faith conviction to form the synergy of Christian education: faith growth.

Needs of Contemporary Persons

Too often we revert to the placement of persons for educational ministry based on the surface knowledge we can obtain from them

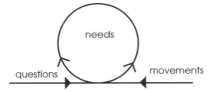

while living and ministering in a world that provides an astounding array of tools to assist in discovering the needs of persons. In this section I want to identify a representative number of those tools. All of them contain a liability that should be noted: Our culture is immersed in the habit of placing persons in stages, phases, and categories. Such a mentality has both healthy and unhealthy applications. With these acknowledgements, I advocate that the core vision for Christian education take these concepts seriously in faith growth.

Summer and Winter Spirituality

In his book *A Cry of Absence*, Martin Marty refers to the spiritual seasons experienced by Christians. An effort is made to remind our hearts of what they may have forgotten: truth can walk through wintertime and summertime. The summertime of the heart is characterized by peace, joy, hope, optimism, and encouragement. The wintertime of the heart is characterized by doubt, turbulence, pessimism, despair, and discouragement.

To some degree each of us knows a winter and summer spirituality, but the concept suggests we have a basic spiritual temperament of one or the other. The difficulty lies in our tendency to be one and demonstrate little sensitivity for understanding the other. The person of a summer spirituality experiences the immediacy of God's presence and knows the peace and joy granted by the presence of the Holy Spirit. The person of a winter spirituality feels deeply scarred by life's experiences and knows the anguish of walking by faith and not by sight. This is not a question of whether or not one is converted, but how one experiences the spiritual life. Sadly, each of these spiritual temperaments tends to look down on the other temperament.[29] In biblical and extrabiblical references, we can identify examples of each:

Summer	Winter
Joseph	Jeremiah
Ruth	Naomi
Peter	John the Baptist
Mary	Martha
St. Francis	Søren Kierkegaard
Robert Schuller	Tony Campolo

Learning Style Inventory

David A. Kolb has developed an instrument that reveals a person's preferences in educational environments. The inventory is "a simple self-description test, based on experimental learning theory, that is designed to measure strengths and weaknesses in a learner."[30] The material is based on the idea that the effective learner relies on four different learning modes:

(1) "concrete experience"—involving oneself openly and without bias in new experiences
(2) "reflective observation"—observing these experiences from many perspectives
(3) "abstract conceptulization"—creating concepts that integrate observations into sound theories
(4) "active experimentation"—using these theories to make decisions and solve problems.[31]

Please Understand Me

Please Understand Me is the title of a volume that offers helpful interpretive material based on the Myers-Briggs type indicators of character and temperament. The Myers-Briggs instrument is an assessment tool concerned with some of the differences in people. These differences result from where individuals like to focus their attention, the way individuals like to take in information, the way individuals like to decide, and the kind of lifestyle individuals adopt.

Because people are different in these fundamental ways, they have different appetites and desires, they approach belief differently, and they judge differently. When I see these differences of individual behavior and preference in you, there is a predictable tendency to attribute those qualities to flaws or weaknesses in you, and you tend to judge me with similar conclusions. But, internally, we each know these differences as an expression of elemental identity.

Each of us may learn to compensate for these dimensions of temperament, but changing a person's basic temperament is an extraordinarily difficult, if not impossible, task. It is more desirable to work within those temperaments than to attempt to change them. The Myers-Briggs instrument and the *Please Understand Me* book utilize a scale of four indicators:

(1) extroversion/introversion
(2) intuition/sensation
(3) thinking/sensation
(4) judging/perceiving[32]

Stages of Faith

Since it was published in 1981, James Fowler's *Stages of Faith* has been appreciated, analyzed, and criticized in many quarters. In this synthesizing work, Fowler pulled together the best work of psychologists, sociologists, theologians, and moral philosophers to delineate the stages of faith. I have found it helpful to assist my students in their faith development by asking two of the crucial questions posed by Fowler:

(1) What are your boundaries of social awareness?
(2) Where is your locus of authority?

The six faith stages are preceded by the stage of primal faith that occurs in infancy:

Stage 1: Intuitive-Projective. Found in early childhood, the features include imagination, stories, and symbols not yet controlled by logical thinking. These images and their associated feelings protect and threaten the individual's life.

Stage 2: Mythic-Literal Faith. Found in childhood and beyond, faith is informed by logical categories of space and time, cause and effect; the person is able to view the world from the perspective of others.

Stage 3: Synthetic-Conventional Faith. Found in adolescence and beyond, identity develops and emotional solidarity with others is possible. This focus is achieved out of an unfocused collection of self-images, values, and beliefs.

Stage 4: Individuative-Reflective Faith. Found in young adulthood and beyond, commitments in relationships and vocation occur as one is able to reflect upon chosen values and beliefs. A person is able to see oneself as a part of a social system and assume appropriate responsibilities in that system.

Stage 5: Conjunctive Faith. Found in midlife and beyond, there is a newfound value assigned to symbol, story, and myth. Life is understood to embrace polarities and paradoxes and multiple interpretations of reality.

Stage 6: Universalizing Faith. Found in midlife of beyond, features include spending the self in love and overcoming division, oppression, and violence with passionate action.[33]

Enneagrams

The word and concept *enneagram* refers to nine points (*ennea* or "nine"; *grammos* or "points"). It employs a nine-pointed star diagram. The enneagram of types is part of an oral teaching tradition. The material is communicated best by seeing and hearing groups of persons of the same type talk about life from their point of view. While the group may appear to be very different on the surface of age, sex, race, and style, their choices, preferences, goals, and histories are quite similar. The world looks very different to each of the nine perspectives.[34]

It is important to emphasize the ways that people differ from one another below the surface. We must learn to appreciate how the people who are close to us live out their lives. The enneagram, however, is not a fixed system. Its interconnecting lines indicate a dynamic movement that predicts the ways in which each type is likely to alter its usual behavior when encountering stress or insecurity. The triangular concept conveys the three forces of active, receptive, and reconciling. Listed below are the nine types, followed by a description of the person who fits the type.

The Perfectionist: critically wise, can be a moral hero, critical of self and others, convinced there is one correct way

The Giver: can be genuinely caring and supportive, wants to be loved and appreciated by becoming indispensable to another person

The Performer: can become an effective leader and a competent promoter who leads winning teams, able to represent winning appearances

The Tragic Romantic: can become capable of helping other people through difficulty; committed to the passionate life; noted by the qualities of sadness, the artistic, and the tragic.

The Observer: can become an ivory-tower elitist who is a superior decision-maker; drained by commitment, so maintains an emotional distance from others and protects privacy

The Devil's Advocate: can become a loyal soldier, great team player, and good friend; fearful and plagued by doubts; identifies with minority causes; generally opposed to authoritarianism

The Epicure: can become skilled at developing theories and finding a synthesis, an adventurer in search of love and eternal youth, happy, stays on an emotional high, stimulating company

The Boss: an excellent leader and can be a powerful supporter for the safe passage of other people, extremely protective, loves a good fight, loves to be in control but can feel respect for a worthy opponent

The Mediator: can become an excellent counselor and peacemaker, sees many perspectives, able to replace personal views with those of others because of knowing the needs of others better than that of self.[35]

This core vision for Christian education is not intended to call for a new basis of grouping and grading, but it is intended as a call for a less-than-superficial understanding of the needs of contemporary persons. To those who might respond to these processes with these questions:

• Do you have any idea how much of a demand this would place on Christian educators?
• Have you acknowledged the complexity this would introduce into structures of educational ministry?

I respond by asking these questions in turn:

• How crucial is our task in the life of the community of faith?
• If we know how to approach our ministry more seriously from a more informed perspective, what is our obligation?
• How much more effectively could we equip and enable a congregation if they and we had some sense of summer/winter spirituality; if they and we had assessed learning styles to inform our expectations; if we had some sensitivities to the universal plea, please understand me; if stages of faith were pursued in our churches with passion; and if we listened to persons talk about life from their points of view?
• What if all of this happened, not in isolation, but in the synergism of questions of faith conviction, movements of educational ministry, and the needs of contemporary persons?

Trends of Contemporary Environments

Convictions are expressions of faith that transcend time. Trends are reflections of the contemporary environment. Movements are causes to which groups subscribe over a span of time.

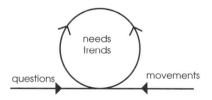

In the 1960s, I served a church consumed with group experiences. Youth retreats were dominated by an activity called "sharing." Adult conferences overflowed with group strategies. Children were told to express themselves in mobiles and collages developed in group activities.

In another church in the early 70s, we were preoccupied with strategies growing out of the psychological concepts of "I'm OK,

You're OK." It seemed that everyone was training to become an amateur religious psychologist.

Later in the 70s, "bus ministry" concepts defined and determined the purpose of children's church, the structure of children's Sunday school, and the booming statistics of church enrollments.

In Sunday School in the 1980s, we experienced the "growth spiral"—followed by "super growth spirals," then "mega," then "ultra."

Trends are ever with us. In themselves, many trends are not harmful; but trends need to be noted for what they are, no more than that. They must be acknowledged if we are to avoid a drunken methodological stupor in educational ministry. In the synergism of faith growth, I call for the acknowledgement of trends and their inevitable influence. But I insist also that it is incumbent upon those who serve as leaders in the church to identify trends and name them for the benefit of those we serve and for the benefit of our spiritual well-being. How can this be done? Here are four steps:

(1) Determine the distinctions between trends and convictions, and trends and movements (note, the earlier sections of this chapter that offered discussions of convictions and movements).
(2) Name trends in your environment, and note their faddish qualities.
(3) Selectively participate in trends that will not be incompatible with your chosen convictions and movements.
(4) Take note when a trend is no longer in fashion, and laugh at your own behavior!

My research has enabled me to identify many examples of trends in tension with movements and convictions in Christian education. I will identify and discuss three of them.

Example 1

Illustration A. In 1978, John Westerhoff became editor of *Religious Education*, the journal of the Religious Education

Association. This journal has sustained an engagement with church- and synagogue-related educators for ninety years. Westerhoff also edited *Who Are We?*, a book of essays reflecting the history of the interests expressed in the journal. Therein, Westerhoff suggested that Ian Knox's typology serves a useful purpose for classifying positions among religious educators. The typology describes immanentists, transcendists, and integrationists.

Immanentists believe that God erupts into human affairs from within the world. With these persons, Westerhoff paired the maturationists who view human nature from the social sciences proceeding along lines of natural growth and development.

Transcendists believe that God erupts into human affairs from outside the world. With these persons, Westerhoff paired the environmentalists who view human nature from theology proceeding along lines that communicate a distinctive heritage and a special revelation.

Integrationists affirm the paradox created by the two positions and advocate a basis for synthesis of the two.[36]

Illustration B. Westerhoff included an article from the 1908 Religious Education Association Convention written by Washington Gladden, a Congregationalist pastor from Ohio. Gladden proposed bringing moral and religious forces into effective educational unity. He identified religion with character and morality and all the moral forces operating at that time in the United States.[37]

*****

Trend or Movement or Conviction? Knox's typology and Gladden's proposals for educational unity are illustrative of movements and trends. I would argue that the typologies are movements because they may be applied in any setting of religious education in almost any culture, at any time. On the other hand, the possibilities of educational unity only lend themselves to certain theological traditions in a limited number of historical and cultural environments. They are trends.

Illustration C. In 1932, Nevin C. Harner expressed the belief that religious education must become a science so that it could command respect and confirm that the scientific spirit is understood as being deeply religious.[38]

Illustration D. H. Shelton Smith, professor of religious education at Duke University Divinity School, wrote an important article for *Religous Education* in 1934. He believed that liberal theology and progressive education had misinformed religious education. Smith adopted the idea that Christian education begins with God and Jesus Christ, not with persons and their values.[39]

*****

Trend or Movement or Conviction? In almost any environment there will be those who subscribe to the thought that science and religion should be connected. Others will protest against such associations. I see the possibilities of understanding this 1932 article as a movement in some expressions and a trend in others. Clearly, the 1934 article reflects a conviction about the centrality of Christian education and the alien features of progressive education.

Illustration E. In 1953, Randolph Crump Miller attempted to establish Christian education as essentially a theological discipline. He thought it should be placed in departments or schools of theology. He also defended the significance of Christian education for the whole ministry of the church rather than for only one aspect of ministry.[40]

Illustration F. Theoretical concerns in religious education have been dominated by white male leaders, primarily in academics. Practical concerns have been left to white and ethnic women. Iris Cully is an exception to that generalization. She wrote an article in 1967 to support the theory of nurturing as a means in Christian education.[41]

*****

Trend or Movement or Conviction? Both Iris Cully and Randolph Crump Miller are sponsoring convictions that transcend time and place. To view Christian education as a theological discipline is much more than a trend. To choose to support Christian nurture over Christian instruction is far more than a fad of the time. Is the contribution of a woman, Iris Cully, given its theoretical and theological concerns, a trend? I think not!

Example 2

Illustration G. A second example of the distinctions between trends and movements and trends and convictions is found in the work of Christian educator Marvin J. Taylor. Taylor edited several introductions to Christian education in the 1960s and the 1970s. Two of those introductions will be utilized to illustrate trends, movements, and convictions as they were expressed by more than twenty different Christian educators.

Though the two books served similar purposes, their titles reflect different environments. The 1966 version is entitled *An Introduction to Christian Education*.[42] In 1976, the title *Foundations for Christian Education in an Era of Change* was chosen.[43] The titles are themselves evidence of trends. The first title suggests stability and an ordered approach. This is demonstrated further by the subsections and grouping of the articles under "Foundations"; "Administration"; "Programs, Methods, Materials"; and "Agencies and Organizations." A decade later, the articles were not submitted to any internal grouping, but reflected some moderate effort given to sequence.

*****

Trend or Movement or Conviction? What evidence exists in the two volumes that faith convictions have been acknowledged? Theological, biblical, and ethical issues are brought into focus in each volume. Each contains articles addressing historical and theoretical convictions. The earlier book devotes separate chapters to psychological, sociocultural, and dialogical perspectives of Christian education. In 1976, those headings were not found, but the movements and trends of developmental approaches, women's studies, values education, liberation theology, and black theology had come to the surface. In 1966, those subjects were not addressed with comparable prominence, if at all. Rather, the movements of denominations, interdenominational cooperation, and nondenominational factors were identified. Again, in 1976, articles on worship, curriculum theory, the ecumenical movement, Western Europe, and the Third World were included. These illustrations point to the movements and trends that shape and guide our perceptions of Christian education in the environments that surround us.

Example 3

Illustration H. For the treatment of "trends of contemporary environments," the third example will compare two unpublished documents that reflect the proceedings of meetings of Southern Baptist Christian educators held in 1967 and 1975. The presentations and discussions of each meeting were dominated by two books. The book that shaped the 1967 meeting was *Preparing Instructional Objectives*, written by Robert Mager.[44] A major paper and workshop were offered with the title: "The Role of Instructional Objectives in Teaching and Training," which reflected the educational movements and trends of the time and the environment in which the meeting was conducted. Today, I know of very few persons who would conclude that instructional objectives are an element of a core vision for faith conviction.[45]

The book that shaped the 1975 meeting was *The Greening of the Church* by Findley Edge.[46] Out of more than forty-five workshops, a dozen leaders and resource persons led discussions devoted to the themes of the book. Those themes included the renewal movement, structural/institutional renewal, and the celebration (not toleration) of differences.[47]

*****

Trend or Movement or Conviction? The record of the 1967 meeting demonstrated a heavy attention to trends and movements and little concern for faith convictions. Where biblical and theological issues were presented, they were isolated monologic events led by scholars from fields other than Christian education.

In the 1975 meeting, trends could be observed in the language of the renewal ideas. Movements of renewal, in fact, have been observed in many periods of church history. Many biblical and theological issues were presented in a monologic fashion. At this meeting, more Christian educators made the presentations. As with the 1967 meeting, the proceedings demonstrated a heavy attention to trends and movements.

A Reflection on Core Vision

In this chapter, I have proposed that the core vision for Christian education should be discovered or recovered in the synergism of faith growth. Questions of faith conviction must be reflected upon. Movements of educational ministry must be understood. The needs of contemporary persons must be assessed. Trends of contemporary environments must be acknowledged. As we are able to engage these elements, we will observe the working together of two or more dynamics that have a greater effect than the sum of their individual effects to grant us a core vision for Christian education.

Notes

[1]Dietrich Bonhoeffer, quoted in Robert Raines, *Creative Brooding* (New York: MacMillan, 1966) 33. I have chosen to use this secondary source to call attention to the formula for devotional material developed by Raines: Contemporary quote from literary source in dialogue with quotes from biblical source in dialogue with prayer thoughts.

[2]C. F. D. Moule, "Children of God," in *The Interpreter's Dictionary of the Bible*, vol. 1, ed. G. A. Buttrick (New York: Abingdon, 1962): 559-61. Hereafter referred to as IDB in all subsequent citations.

[3]Walker Percy, *Sign Posts in a Strange Land* (New York: Noonday Press, 1991) 136.

[4]W. A. Quanbeck, "Forgiveness," in *IDB*, vol. 2, 314-19.

[5]Charles F. Poole, *Don't Cry Past Tuesday* (Macon Ga: Smyth & Helwys, 1991) 94-95.

[6]Gordon Cosby, *Handbook for Mission Groups* (Waco TX: Word, 1975) 94-95. In my experience, these three functions have been embodied with inspiring vitality by the Church of the Savior in Washington, D. C. As a Christian educator, I shall always be indebted to them for allowing their faith convictions to permeate their ecclesial structure.

[7]Elizabeth O'Connor, *Journey Inward, Journey Outward* (New York: Harper & Row, 1968) 10, 16, 24.

[8]Findley B. Edge, *A Quest for Vitality in Religion* (Nashville TN: Broadman, 1963; rev. ed. Macon GA: Smyth & Helwys, 1995) 9-14. In this book we are warned of the dangers inherently present in the forces of institutional power. It is imperative that every generation takes those warnings seriously in the ministry of Christian education.

[9]Fyodor Dostoevsky, *The Brother's Karamazov*, trans. Constance Garnett, Great Books of the Western World, vol. 52 (Chicago: Encyclopedia Britannica, 1952) 130.

[10]Dante Aligheri, *The Divine Comedy*, trans. Charles E. Norton, Great Books of the Western World, vol. 21 (Chicago: Encyclopedia Britannica, 1952) 4.

[11]Freeman Dyson, *Disturbing the Universe* (New York: Harper Colophon, 1979) 52-53.

[12]*New York Public Library Book of Twentieth-Century American Quotations* (New York: Warner Books, 1992) 379.

[13]Karl Rahner, *Hearer of the Word* (New York: Herder & Herder, 1969) 87.

[14]Thomas Merton, *Contemplation in a World of Action* (New York: Saturday Review Press, 1971) 145.

[15]J. A. Wharton, "Shema," in *IDB* vol. 4, 320-22.

[16]Thomas H. Groome, *Christian Religious Education* (San Francisco: Harper & Row, 1980) 136.

[17]Evelyn Stagg & Frank Stagg, *Woman in the World of Jesus* (Philadelphia: Westminster, 1978). This research has served a pivotal role in my understanding of the issue of women in ministry.

[18]Lewis J. Sherrill, *The Rise of Christian Education* (New York: MacMillan, 1944). While it is true that the research in this volume is limited, I have found the book and its consciousness of Christian education to be instructive.

[19]Edge, 35-37.

[20]M. H. Pope, "Way," in *IDB*, vol. 4, 817-18.

[21]W. A. Quanbeck, "Confession" in *IDB*, vol. 1, 667-68.

[22]James Reed and Ronnie Prevost, *A History of Christian Education* (Nashville TN: Broadman and Holman, 1993) 79.

[23]Ibid., 85.

[24]Sherrill, 160-63.

[25]Ibid., 142-68.

[26]Max Weber, *The Protestant Ethic and the Spirit of Capitalism*, trans. Talcott Parsons (New York: Charles Scribner's Sons, 1958). I have concluded that any view of Calvinism must engage in a dialogue with this book and its amazing sociological commentary before a view can claim to be informed.

[27]Robert Henderson, *The Teaching Office in the Reformed Tradition* (Philadelphia: Westminster, 1962) 33.

[28]Robert Lynn and Elliott Wright, *The Big Little School* (New York: Harper & Row, 1971). This book is small, but the research is impressive. The authors allowed their historical perspective to be shaped by such subjects as "the music of the Sunday School movement."

[29]Martin E. Marty, *A Cry of Absence* (San Francisco: Harper & Row, 1983).

[30]David A. Kolb, *Learning Style Inventory* (Boston: McBer and Co., 1976) 5.

[31]Ibid.

[32]David Kiersey and Marilyn Bates, *Please Understand Me* (Del Mar NY : Prometheus Book Co., 1984) 13-22.

[33]James W. Fowler, *Stages of Faith* (San Francisco: Harper & Row, 1981).

[34]Helen Palmer, *Enneagram* (San Francisco: Harper Collins, 1988) 5.

[35]Ibid., 7.

[36]John Westerhoff, ed. *Who Are We? The Quest for a Religious Education* (Birmingham AL: Religious Education Press, 1978) 7.

[37]Ibid., 23-33.

[38]Ibid., 83-96.

[39]Ibid., 97-109.

[40]Ibid., 110-22.

[41]Ibid., 150-64.

[42]Marvin J. Taylor, ed. *An Introduction to Christian Education* (Nashville TN: Abingdon, 1966).

[43]Marvin J. Taylor, ed., *Foundations for Christian Education in an Era of Change* (Nashville TN: Abingdon, 1976).

[44]Robert F. Mager, *Preparing Instructional Objectives* (Palo Alto CA: Fearon Publishers, 1962).

[45]"Proceedings of the 47th Annual Meeting of the Southwestern Baptist Religious Education Association," August 1967.

[46]Findley B. Edge, *The Greening of the Church* (Waco TX: Word, 1971).

[47]"National Conference on Church Educational Ministry," February 1975.

Curricular Tasks

S uppose we have the luxury of designing a program structure for a congregation "from the ground up." We have been given permission to think creatively and constructively without being blindly faithful to the past or unfaithful to our heritage. We have been charged to be both relevant and traditional. Would you choose a formula that gives dominance to Bible study opportunities and neglect experiences in worship, community, or discipleship? Probably not. Most of us would move toward a church program that incorporates all four dimensions in the curricular task.

Analogously, a cow must have an adequate skeletal structure to be identifiable as a cow. At the same time, it is understandable that a cow with a protruding or visible skeletal structure is a sick cow. In a similar image, the curricular task must have an adequate institutional presence to be identifiable. At the same time, curriculum can be absorbed with itself and the curricular structure so self-evident that it represents a kind of institutional sickness. The curricular task must reflect an institutional presence and a relational sensitivity. The following diagram is an effort to move toward a vision of Christian education that embodies all four of the curricular tasks in a holistic model. That model then offers a synergism of relational and institutional needs.[1] Note that in this description of the body of Christ, horizontal and vertical lines are rare. Circular lines dominate the graphic.

The center circle offers worship envisioned at the heart of faith growth. In the second circle the faith community gathers to warm its ecclesiastical hands at the theological fire of worship. The third ring calls for the covenant community to engage in the study of the biblical and extrabiblical witnesses. In the outer ring is one word that represents the witness, ministry, and service of discipleship. This graphic will serve as a cross section of the church in this statement of the curricular task of Christian education.

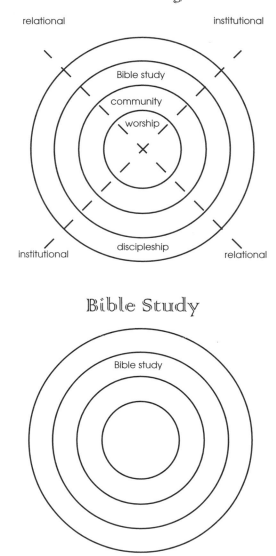

Bible Study

Question: How is it best for Christian educators to view the curricular task of Bible study?

Answer: It is best to view it from the perspective of those who are qualified both as biblical scholars and Christian educators.

Where do we find such perspectives? I have two sources to nominate for consideration. First is the "Christian Faith and Life Curriculum: A Program for Church and Home," designed by James D. Smart, the Jesup Professor of Biblical Interpretation at Union Theological Seminary in New York City, and developed by the United Presbyterian Church, U.S.A.[2]

In one volume, Smart focused on "the strange silence of the Bible in the church." He accused conservatives of silencing the Bible by worshiping it as an idol. Conversely, he accused liberals of ignoring the Bible and silencing it. He acknowledged that teaching and preaching the Bible is a much more complex task in the environment of critical methods of Bible study. Smart also acknowledged a number of other factors contributing to biblical ignorance:

• "A Bible that is left in the medieval world and a [church] membership that has moved on into the [contemporary] world."[3]
• The religious publishing houses and church leaders have been reluctant to allow critical problems of the biblical text to be discussed in literature provided for Bible study. "The consequences of leaving a twentieth-century church with a seventeenth-century mind were ignored."[4]
• "The authority of Scripture comes particularly into question because blind obedience to it only too often in the past has been used to fasten upon people attitudes that eventually turned out to be unchristian."[5] This has been illustrated when church leaders have used the Bible to defend racism.
• "The exploration of cultures and religions other than our own has shown a fair measure of wisdom distributed among them all. No nation has had truth or goodness for its private preserve."[6]
• "Much of the difficulty that surrounds this problem of biblical authority has arisen from the attempt of church leaders to make God's authority visible, tangible, and incontestable in a way that it never was for prophets or apostles or Jesus himself."[7]

Another source for viewing the curricular task of Bible study is the published thought of Mary C. Boys. She is the Skinner and

McAlpin Professor of Practical Theology at Union Theological Seminary in New York City. She holds that the Bible must have a dominant role in Christian education.[8] Boys informs church educators with her analysis of biblical interpretation and its relationship to the curricular task.

For Mary Boys, the junction of theological and educational approaches is the location of the formation of Christian education. She also delineates the evidence of a new attitude toward the Bible in our society. We have come from a time when the text of the available translation could be taken at face value, to a contemporary time when we read the Bible and appropriately ask, "What really happened?" and "What might all of this mean today?"[9]

Boys identifies five related sets of concerns undergirding the contemporary approach to the Bible:

(1) "Relevance—How can the Bible, an ancient document, speak to current concerns?"
(2) "Communicability—How does one grasp what an earlier age with a different mentality thought?"
(3) "Limitations—In what sense do biblical injunctions and stories transcend their particularity?"
(4) "Normativity—What is the authority of the Bible in regard to issues . . . simply outside the scope of the biblical authors?"
(5) "Obligation—How can the power of the Word be heard anew in the [contemporary world]?"[10]

On the current scene, Mary Boys observes the chasm between Christian education and biblical scholarship. Among the causes for this chasm, she lists the complex tools of biblical criticism that bewilder Christian educators and other nonspecialists. She also identifies the turbulence that critical methods of Bible study insinuate into devotional methods of Bible study. In this turmoil, Mary Boys offers this refreshing affirmation: "The Bible is above all else the church's book: it is not the exclusive property of a professional guild of scholars."[11]

She proposes that we prize both the expertise of the scholar and the wisdom of the servant. The servant may indeed bring special gifts to biblical interpretation. Boys writes:

> Listening is an art, not learned primarily in graduate school. . . . Those who work with children, the elderly, or the handicapped may well have refined this ability far beyond the most learned articulate scholar[12]

Biblical interpretation is facilitated by those who are able to listen. The Christian educator's skills are most valuable in the process of synergy. They bring theological views under scrutiny to determine their educational implications, and they filter educational views to decipher their theological compatibilities. It is not adequate for the Christian educator to possess knowledge of theological content and separate knowledge of educational strategy. The knowledge must have the possibility of becoming news. Synergism of the content and strategy must work together to produce faith growth.

James Smart, writing at the midpoint of this century, proposed that Christian educators have a responsibility in helping other believers understand "how the Bible becomes contemporary." He was convinced that "the Bible itself is a massive demonstration of how Scripture becomes contemporary."[13] The one dynamic that remained constant over the millennia was the covenant relationship between God and God's people. There was always a community of some size that preserved the story of God's dealings with Christian believers. That covenant has had a resiliency to redefine itself in multiple contexts.

Church history also provides a variety of examples of the Bible becoming contemporary. Most dramatically, this is demonstrated in the Protestant Reformation. The biblical scholar and Christian educator, James Smart, proposed that we must live in two worlds. Immersion in the world of the biblical material must be joined by an immersion in our own world. Smart wrote:

> The two worlds come together so that the Scriptures are like a magic glass through which we look to see ourselves [and others] and our world as they really are. . . . Far too often we look into the Bible and see only what is in the Bible. . . . We have never looked past the words to the word of God.[14]

Clearly, Mary Boys emerges as an informed and experienced contemporary guide for Christian educators when she insists that we avoid the habit of equating Christian education with concepts of formal schooling. When that association is allowed to shape our expectation, several harmful eventualities may occur. The association of the two can cause us to miss the educational component in preaching, counseling, social action, or worship. Also we can miss the Christian curriculum that should be woven into the fabric of daily routines and events.

As Christian educators, we have the predictable responsibility of coordinating corporate programs of Bible study for groups. We also need to develop a sense of responsibility to encourage individuals to embody approaches to private Bible study for personal enrichment. Subsequent books in this series will address the strategies and approaches for Bible study. In this vision statement, I want to emphasize both group and private approaches to Bible study.

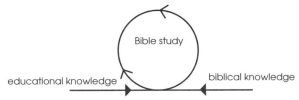

Both Mary Boys and James Smart offer the synergetic understanding depicted. The inadequacy of Christian education and its attention to Bible study is exposed when either biblical knowledge or educational knowledge are neglected. Each is called into dialogue in faith growth.

Discipleship

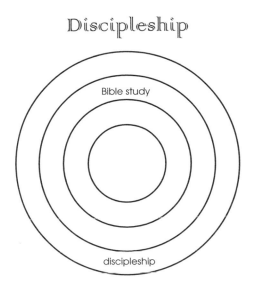

Let me reaffirm the statement in the introduction to this book and the opening paragraphs of this chapter. The four curricular tasks are not programs primarily, but rather constant needs in the congregation that demand the attention of the Christian educator. In the outer ring of the graphic appears the word discipleship. It represents the witness, ministry, and service of the Christian servant-leader. The concept of a servant-leader is difficult to express in any context. It is enormously difficult to communicate when Christian groups are led by authoritarian, dictatorial leaders.

Hermann Hesse's story *Journey to the East* tells of a band of pilgrims on a mythical journey to the East.[15] With them is the servant Leo, who does their daily chores, sustains them with his spirit and, by the quality of his presence, lifts them to be more than they thought they could be. The journey is meaningful for each pilgrim in a unique way until Leo disappears. Then everything seems to deteriorate. After wandering for some years, the narrator is taken into the Order that sponsored the journey to the East. To the narrator's astonishment, Leo is revealed to be the leader of the Order, its guiding spirit.

Leo portrays two roles at once. He is the servant who, by acting with integrity and spirit, builds trust and lifts people, helping
them to grow. He also is the leader who is trusted to shape the
lives of others by going ahead and showing the way.

Robert Greenleaf has identified additional characteristics of
the servant-leader. The attributes described by Greenleaf parallel
the descriptions of Jesus in the New Testament. I believe that they
coalesce to provide a superlative description of the qualities of
discipleship.

• *Foresight* is the ability to be historian, contemporary analyst, and
prophet in selected moments; the disciple can see and express the
connectedness of our lives in Christ.
• *Healing* requires the understanding that the search for wholeness is always being sought by those who help and those who
would be helped; it is the same idea as the "wounded healer."
• *Withdrawal* represents the ability to reorient oneself, to sort out
priorities, and to pace oneself.
• *Listening* begins with attention, involves a searching spirit,
requires discipline, and is also an attitude.
• *Acceptance* suggests interest in and affection for those disciples
who journey with us; but it is clearly an accepting spirit that
believers and nonbelievers do not have to deserve or earn.[16]

I find a collection of fascinating parallels when comparing these
qualities and stories with the biblical story from Luke 24.

In this vision for Christian education, our concern is not centered on the strategies or organization for discipleship so much as
it centered on the qualities and characteristics of discipleship.
There are varied biblical meanings of the word disciple. Essentially, it is a reference to a learner or pupil. Moses, the Pharisees,
and John the Baptist mention their disciples in biblical references.
More than twenty references are made to the disciples of Christ in
the book of Acts. The Gospels contain the use of the word more
than 200 times.[17] Pierson Parker writes:

In Matthew and Luke, it appears only on Jesus' lips. There, it is in teachings about the nature of discipleship. . . . Indeed, full discipleship and full Christlikeness are the same thing (Luke 6:40).[18]

Along with the biblical guidelines, my understanding of the concept of discipleship is informed by three literary archetypes. Robert A. Johnson offers profound insight on this subject through his analysis of three literary figures: Don Quixote, Hamlet, and Faust.[19]

In the story of Don Quixote, we reflect on the person of simple consciousness who lives in a secure world of internal happiness and optimism. Quixote is aware that the external world needs to be altered, but he has no idea what that world is like or how it works. He pursues his ideas and visions, by "tilting at windmills."

An opposing posture is taken by Hamlet. His consciousness is complex. He is painfully aware of a realistic knowledge of the external world. Hamlet is worried, anxious, and nostalgic. He recognizes division and tragedy in his environment. That recognition induces paralysis internally; he cannot make up his mind—"he knows too little to be made whole."[20]

Faust represents a synergism of these two literary figures. He portrays an enlightened consciousness that accepts both paradox and synthesis. The disciple, Faust, works on a translation of the Gospel of John. He concludes that a central meaning of "In the beginning was the Word" may be rendered, "In the beginning was the Act." His insight is a reminder: we must act upon our knowledge for it to become news. At the beginning of the story, Faust is weak and frightened, and the shadow, Mephistopheles, is ruthless and bold. Over the years of dialogue between the two, Faust becomes strong, and Mephistopheles has learned to love.

For our interest in Christian discipleship, I find several clues in these literary archetypes. I believe that some theologians have a quixotic image in mind when they reflect on "first naivete." The central dynamic of revelation for Christians is the incarnation. The incarnate Christ demonstrates equal validity given to the human and the divine. Faust is driven to a dialogue with the source of consciousness and power: the spiritual world of the sacred and the holy. The center of consciousness is relocated from the ego to a center greater than one's self. Hamlet represents the paralysis that comes from endless analysis.

In extrabiblical sources, I have not identified a more dramatic or engaging description of the chapters that move us toward discipleship than that provided by Frederick Buechner. He suggests three chapters of spirituality that are common for each disciple in the Christian tradition. He employs poetical language to identify the three: (1) once below a time, (2) once upon a time, and (3) once beyond time.[21]

"Once below a time" refers to the span of time from birth until the individual discovers that the adults in the person's world are not in control of the world. In my own life, it seems to me that the discovery about the powerlessness of the adults in my world happened during World War II. When I was six years of age, my father was sent to combat on a troop train. My mother and I had not been given the opportunity of saying goodbye to my father. We only knew that the troop train would pass within two blocks of our home on a particular day of the week. We sat by the railroad all day and into the evening, waiting and hoping. Did we see my father? As a child, I convinced myself that I saw him waving from a speeding rail car. That experience was conclusive. I learned that the adults in my world were not in control of the world! For me, once below a time was coming to an end.

My own acknowledgement of powerlessness happened when I realized that I, as a newly commissioned officer in the U.S. Marine Corps, had not been prepared to handle the ethical questions of violence and warfare. No one in my family, my church, or my education had led me to grapple with the ethical issues raised for a Christian in military service. When I confessed my spiritual dilemma with senior officers, I found neither answers nor condemnation. I found those experienced leaders joining me in the questions! In 1962, in a shattering and sobering encounter, I acknowledged that our only hope is in the power of a transcendent and incarnate God. Once upon a time was coming to an end for me. Buechner suggests that a mature discipleship begins when we move into the chapter, "Once beyond time!"

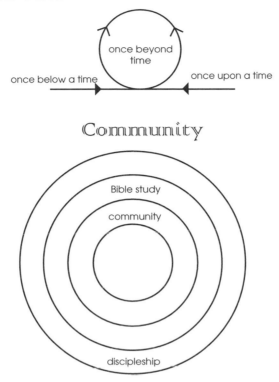

Community

We do not build community by working deliberately and overtly "to build community." When a group experiences community in its most meaningful form of faith community, it is a gift. It is not programmed; rather it grows out of the commitment to serve a larger purpose. It is granted to those disciples who discover or recover a mission more significant than their individual or collective agendas. It is a quality visited upon those who journey toward a "city whose builder and maker is God" (Heb 11:10).

Earlier I emphasized the "Shema" in Deuteronomy 6. Built into that passage is the concept of religious nurture embedded in daily activities (for example, "when you rise up, when you go out, when you come in, when you lie down"). Among the Hebrews, this pattern of daily reflection expanded to note the religious significance of the larger chapters of life or what we may refer to as "rites of passage."

"How do we build community?" I am prepared with a positive response and proposal. In the commitment to observe the rites of passage in our lives, the gift of community is granted. When we celebrate or grieve with one another, we recover the more significant issues of life. When the faith community takes the time to note the large sweeping chapters of individual lives, the quality of our religious family is enriched in a profound and mysterious fashion.

As an indispensable element of this vision of Christian education, I advocate the inclusion of rites of passage in the curriculum of Christian education. For the nuclear family, those rites include: birth, new home, new job, shared meals, marriage, anniversaries, retirement, death. For the church family, those rites are: conversion, baptism, new church home, communion, ordination, commissioning.

If we subscribe to the thought that Christian educators should give their attention to the curricular task both in the biological family and in the congregational family, then rites of passage are a reasonable focus for religious nurture. If the biblical injunctions of the Shema and other scriptural concepts are going to guide us, then marking the stages of a person's advance through life is an obvious channel for Christian education.

The danger in the nuclear family is that these passages can be noted with such hurried casualness that their importance is barely evident. When a death occurs in a family, Christian educators have a responsibility to equip and enable families to reflect on the values of the deceased person, to rehearse the story of that person's life, and to acknowledge the pain and joy of those memories. At the passage of a move into different housing, Christian educators have a responsibility to help persons celebrate the new surroundings and the possibilities that new neighbors offer for witness, ministry, and service.

In the church family, however, these passages can be noted with such preoccupations that their significance is devalued. Too often, the newly baptized person carries memories of the depth or temperature of the water and little more! What if Christian educators led congregations to see that baptism is a wonderful opportunity to reflect on all the influences that have operated in the person's life to bring them to the baptismal waters? What are the possibilities in faith growth if Christian educators not only encourage congregations to find significant transactions of commissioning persons to enter into congregational life, but also challenge congregations to commission persons to leave one congregation and enter the life of another church? Although these illustrations are not intended to be strategies to build community, I believe that community happens when larger issues are pursued. The gift of community is granted when the discipline of study or mission has consumed disciples in the Christian tradition.

The curricular task of community is not significant primarily because it brings the dynamic of energy and vitality to a group. A community carries messages and values with or without our recognition. Communities are a vital component of the curricular task of Christian education. Donald Miller provides a perspective on the nature of community related to this.

(1) "All communities give their members a basic perspective on the world."[22] In the first chapter I reminded you of the story of the apostle Peter in Acts 10. The early Christian community had given him a perspective of provincialism. His encounter with the "unapproved world" allowed the spirit of God to convict Peter of his narrow view and encourage him toward a more inclusive view. Peter's experience, in turn, has altered the perspective held by Christian communities through the ages. Given the perspectives of the community of faith that nurtured you during your formative years, which views do you affirm, reject, or modify now? Given the perspectives of the community of faith in which you presently serve, what basic perspectives do you knowingly communicate in Christ's name? What basic perspectives might you unknowingly communicate in the name of Christ?

(2) "All communities give their members a basic emotional orientation."[23] A community orients toward one of two polarities. At one extreme are the emotional qualities of faith, hope, love, humility, courage, hospitality, and gratitude. At the other extreme are the emotional qualities of hatred, greed, jealousy, suspicion, and self-righteousness. What are you doing in your congregation to affirm the produce that grows out of the spirit of God? This is a concern of faith growth.

(3) "All communities give their members a basic expressive language."[24] How have the words, "the kingdom of God," shaped us? There is an image of God and God's people that is compatible with monarchical language. God is a loving and just king who is all-knowing and all-controlling. This association of God with a monarchy and the church with a kingdom has its biblical sources in both the Old and New Testaments (see, for example, Job 40, 41; Matt 19; Rom 9).

Other views in the Bible present a different image of the church and God (see Isa 53, 63; Phil 2). Here is a vulnerable image of God. This view cherishes the gentleness of God. It is in love and pity that God redeems us. God is present in our affliction. The expressive language for those views is found in the concept of the "Suffering Servant" to refer to God, and the "household of faith" to refer to the church.

These days we hear and read about "politically correct" language. Political correctness is not the issue here. The issue is that those who are defined by others who have power are taking that power away from the definers. Some Christian leaders have an appetite for "kingdom of God" language when they speak for God; they enjoy the power to define, which gives them control. Other Christians are taking that power away by choosing the expressive language of the "household of faith."

(4) "All communities give their members certain common values."[25] In the face of the cultural values of the early church, Jesus taught the values of loving God and loving others as we love ourselves. Jesus spoke against the values of that contemporary society: the love of power, the love of wealth, and the love of domination. It is a common value for the Christian witness to be

countercultural in any age. What counter cultural values do you communicate in the curriculum of your community of faith? What cultural values can you afford to communicate and yet be faithful to your faith convictions?

Donald Miller offers this concluding remark concerning the nature of community as a curricular task:

> All communities give their members a certain way of relating to people which stands between trust and mistrust, generosity and rejection, respect and control, inclusion and exclusion.[26]

Worship

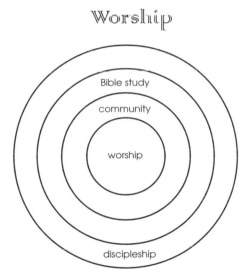

Should Christians be trained to worship? One response is that such training is possible and desirable. Another response is that it is not possible to devise training to worship! Each response contains an element of truth.

In the affirmative response, worship training is possible by noting the obvious. Individually, we were not born with a set of convictions about that which is appealing and unappealing in styles of worship. What then is the source for personal preferences regarding styles of worship? What informs these stereotypical reactions?

- "It was an excellent sermon!"
- "I loved the special music this morning!"
- "Our worship service continues to be boring!"
- "Everything we did in worship was psychological, relevant, and incomprehensible!"
- "I can make it through another week because of our worship services!"
- "Most public worship is a drop of intellectualism in a sea of emotionalism!"

Obviously, a person's experience in his or her formative years is enormously influential within such statements. The worship experiences of childhood set the standards by which we judge subsequent encounters. Developmentally, we have been imbued with a style of worship because we were more susceptible at certain stages of life. In specific periods of development we were primed to react and rebel toward alternate styles of worship. Henry Horn makes this observation:

> This seems to be so obvious that it is difficult to see how we have so completely ignored education in worship in our churches. . . . We merely assume that the forms will automatically catch hold of people in their use.[27]

Exposure to a variety of worship forms is a significant method of training and education. A narrow band of worship experiences will produce a restricted range of appreciation. On one hand, when the exposure to public worship has been circumscribed by regional habit and preference, alternative forms may be threatening and suspect. On the other hand, exposure to a broad range of worship styles may enlarge and enrich the vision of the God we worship. Corporate worship experience with other Christian traditions can awaken us to larger visions of the Creator.

When my grandmother died, her Baptist children and grandchildren deferred to her Roman Catholic heritage and practice by asking the Catholic priest to lead the funeral service. Several of the Baptist children were uncomfortable, if not irritated, by the different pattern of worship in the Catholic funeral observance. Decades later, several of her Baptist grandchildren reflected on that event we had encountered as teenagers. We discovered that some shared fond memories of the funeral service. Cherished images were lovingly rehearsed. In that worship experience great leaps of understanding had occurred for us. Other family members, however, could not recall the event with positive connotations. Exposure to various worship styles runs the risk of each reaction. We may be driven with new appreciation back into our own pattern or tradition. We may be propelled outward into an appreciation for alternate patterns or traditions.

We are trained in worship by our view of the church year. Our view may be shaped because of our exposure to a promotional calendar, or we may be conditioned by a liturgical calendar. In the promotional calendar, corporate worship proceeds from "Witness Commitment Day" to "Make Your Will Month" to "Start a Church Commitment Day" to "Annual Church Council Planning Month" to "Promotion Day." In the liturgical calendar, corporate worship proceeds from Advent to Epiphany to Lent to Holy Week to Pentecost. The vocabulary of the first seems to be more comfortable and satisfying to some persons. The vocabulary of the second seems to be more substantive and appealing to other persons.

As the leaders of a congregation approached the Christmas season and planned for corporate worship, they struggled with the desire to promote the Lottie Moon Christmas offering for foreign missions and the desire to give public emphasis to the four weeks of Advent. Each of these emphases has its place and significance. Each theme represents one of the two calendars. Negotiating a pattern of public worship that is acceptable to each appetite represents a challenge to the respective preferences, their convictions, and their conditioning processes.

Many persons who have their roots and practice in a conservative, evangelical tradition understand the negative answer to the question, "Should Christians be trained to worship?" Specifically, they know you can't "train" for worship. They are suspicious that cold sterility is the result of training in worship. They believe that a certain "woodenness" will accompany deliberate planning for worship. They are sure that the shortest route to snuffing out the vitality of worship is a printed order of worship. They fear the imprint of "professionals" who plan worship.

In a competing attitude, a flawed half step has been taken by ministers who value planning the worship but whose motivation is one of control rather than intentionality. Allowing for spontaneity (for example, testimonies and prayer requests) is threatening. Charismatic and Pentecostal images hover on their view of the horizon. Yearning for stability, these persons agree that the laity cannot be trained for worship. Training pales into subtle forms of manipulation and control. Televised versions of corporate worship are a wonderful handmaiden to this conviction. The time allotted for a prayer or a hymn must be reined in by the ordained hands of professionals who "know" how to lead in public worship.

Other dissenters may be found among those who embody the conviction that training for worship is inappropriate. It is their custom to refrain from dependency on an employed minister. They want to avoid a tendency to "plan" worship and "lead" worship, thereby assuring a freedom and spontaneity in corporate worship.

This section is written with these twin convictions:

(1) True corporate worship may be enhanced by training; it is compatible with an appropriate discipline and order.
(2) True corporate worship is a gift that is neither earned nor deserved; it is compatible with grace and freedom.[28]

The writer Annie Dillard has set the image for a dynamic understanding of worship in these words:

> It is madness to wear ladies' straw hats and velvet hats to church; we should all be wearing crash helmets. Ushers should issue life preservers and signal flares; they should lash us to our pews.[29]

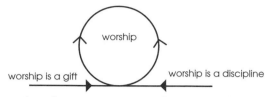

There are educational opportunities inherent with any corporate worship experience. Christian educators have a predictable interest in those opportunities. There are those who have drawn the erroneous conclusion that such an interest springs from territorial designs harbored by the Christian educator. Given my position that the curriculum of the church is inclusive of Bible study, discipleship, community, and any other element that would represent comprehensiveness and connectedness, worship must be included in the curricular tasks of faith growth.

At least one other motive is operating to stimulate the Christian educator's curricular interest in corporate worship. Most worship experiences contain symbols. I am thinking of the symbols of an open Bible, the placement of the pulpit, the communion table, the art associated with the baptistry, hymnals, and Christian pictures that may be found in the images of stained glass or art glass. The Christian educator knows that symbols are instructive. They teach both the inquisitive mind and the wandering mind. We know that we are multisensory beings. The messages conveyed to us most meaningfully are those that engage more than one of our senses. Too often the guiding assumption is that hearing the word means that the mouth and ear are the organs of salvation. That misguided assumption ignores what we learn through the totality of our sensory agents. Faith growth affirms the whole gospel for the whole person. Worship offers many opportunities for knowledge to become news.

A number of challenges seem appropriate for this perspective of worship as a curricular task of Christian education:

• If you cannot devote a significant portion of one corporate worship to each new convert to Christian faith, your congregation has misplaced priorities.

• If you cannot devote a significant portion of one corporate worship to each person departing from membership in your church, your congregation is thinking too small.

• If you cannot devote a significant portion of one corporate worship to persons in your church family who are experiencing rites of passage, your congregation is missing the point.

• If you cannot devote a significant portion of corporate worship to include an opportunity to hear the reading of letters from scattered pilgrims, both historical and contemporary, you are ignoring an apostolic church pattern.

A Reflection on Curricular Tasks

In the local congregation, every minister functions as a curricular advisor in Christian education. Here, I am not speaking of the activity in which a minister places a literature order. If you think that you are fulfilling your curricular responsibility in that activity, you are wrong! In the same fashion, you would be ill-advised to think of yourself as a producer of fruit because you go to the grocery store and select fruit based on judgments you make about mellowness, crispness, color, and juiciness. As you know, those who produced the fruit for your selection were called upon to make judgments about sunshine and rain, heat and cold, bees and blossoms, soils and diseases, fertilizers and sprays, hired hands and wages, and market prices and costs. As a curricular advisor in Christian education, you are expected to exercise the judgments comparable to those of the farmer, not those of the grocery shopper!

Perhaps several other parallel examples would be helpful. You are not the spectator attending the play; you are the critic who analyzes this cast, this director, and this version of the play to enrich and expand the enjoyment and discernment of the audience. In a third image, you are not tracing maps on tracing paper, meticulously copying existing and authoritatively produced maps that have been given to you. You are helping others create their maps for their journeys acting out of a combination of authoritative and experiential maps.[30]

To select from among curricular alternatives in Christian education requires a shift in the range and depth of judgments demanded. The integrity of your ministry dictates that you move from the posture and function of a shopper to a farmer, from a spectator to a critic, and from a map-tracer to a cartographer.

Notes

[1]Among a dozen significant mentors in my life, J. P. Allen would be identified. He has nurtured my understanding of a cross-section of the church in his sermons. Contemporary Christian educators will also recognize the influence of the curricular thought of Maria Harris.

[2]C. K. Ikeler, "James D. Smart," in *Harper's Encyclopedia of Religious Education*, eds. Iris V. Cully and Kendig B. Cully (San Francisco: Harper & Row, 1990) 591.

[3]James D. Smart, *The Strange Silence of the Bible in the Church* (Philadelphia: Westminster, 1970) 65.

[4]Ibid., 67.

[5]Ibid., 92.

[6]Ibid., 42.

[7]Ibid., 98.

[8]Mary C. Boys, *Biblical Interpretation in Religious Education* (Birmingham AL: Religious Education Press, 1980) 1-2.

[9]Ibid., 294-95.

[10]Ibid., 295-96.

[11]Ibid., 299.

[12]Ibid., 320.

[13]Smart, 152.

[14]Ibid., 163.

[15]Hermann Hesse, *Journey to the East*, trans. Unterm Rad (New York: Farrar, Straus, and Giroux, 1968).

[16]Robert K. Greenleaf, *Servant Leadership* (New York: Paulist Press, 1977) 1-16.

[17]Pierson Parker, "Disciple," in *IDB*, vol. 1, 845.

[18]Ibid.

[19]Robert A. Johnson, *Transformation* (San Francisco: Harper Collins, 1991).

[20]Ibid., 38.

[21]Frederick Buechner, *The Sacred Journey* (San Francisco: Harper & Row, 1982).

[22]Donald E. Miller, *Story and Context* (Nashville TN: Abingdon, 1987) 160-61.

[23]Ibid., 161.

[24]Ibid.

[25]Miller, 162.

[26]Ibid., 163.

[27]Henry E. Horn, *Worship in Crisis* (Philadelphia: Fortress, 1972) 143.

[28]William B. Rogers, "Education for Worship," *Review and Expositor*, vol. 65 (1988): 43-49.

[29]Annie Dillard, *Teaching a Stone to Talk* (New York: Harper & Row, 1982) 40.

[30]William B. Rogers, "Curriculum Alternatives for Christian Education," *Review and Expositor*, vol. 90 (1993): 475-86.

Church Functions and Groupings

Functions

Administration

There are many forces, such as marketing strategies, that influence administrative functions in a congregation. The administrative leadership of the community of faith, however, should be anchored to "questions of faith conviction" as a dimension of the core vision. To illustrate, I refer you to chapter 1 and the discussion of accountability. We know how to enlist people to belong to church organizations with an appropriate level of loyalty. The task in the body of Christ, though, is to engage persons to pursue disciplines of mature accountability that include but also extend beyond the congregational organization.

To administer Christian education properly we must reflect on the "movements of educational ministry" as developed in the first chapter. The Christian educator who serves in an administrative role should insist on periodic reflections in light of the story of Peter in Acts 10. For example, how does the structural presence of the congregation challenge the members and participants to be open to acknowledge provincial blind spots that might afflict us and our witness?

Obviously, the third dynamic in the synergism of the core vision, addressing the needs of contemporary persons, is properly implemented and monitored by the administrative function. The administrator must identify and utilize tools that assess the needs of contemporary persons; then the administrator must let the incorporation of that assessment create the appropriate structure. Structural form should follow the function that grows out of the synergistic dialogue described in the first chapter.

Expressions of the administrative function in Christian education are vulnerable to the fickleness of fads and trends. We may participate in trends as they are compatible with our convictions. In terms of leadership, the goal is to name a trend, and call it what it is.

Witness

We are called to be a people who witness to the power of God. That power forgives sin, transforms our society, renews our communities, and brings a new quality of hope to life. Because Jesus is the one through whom all life can be made new, we speak of our loyalty to Jesus. But we are to do more than speak; we are to act out of our loyalty to Jesus.

"The servant Christian is also a Christian witness," as Robert Raines said.[1] We need to learn that the world itself raises the question of faith conviction when our ministry and service are offered in Christian love. The Christian who is first a servant will find a witnessing opportunity located in the relationships created by that servanthood. At times this is called, "Why are you doing this for me, evangelism?". Raines proposed three distinctives of Christian witness that grow out of service. These distinctives are found in the motivation, the resources, and the community of Christian witness.

Out of our reverence for and gratitude to the Lord of life, we are motivated to become Christian servants. Because Christ has served us, we serve others in the name of Christ. We go because we are commissioned to go.

We work out of our own resources and other resources beyond us. We have found forgiveness and hope that provide adequate resource for our witness.

We come from a relationship with other Christians who understand and support us. We are not involved in witness, ministry, and service out of some lonely, singular experience, but rather from our experience of Christian community.[2]

We must be found before we can find. Persons must be served before becoming servants. Likewise, the church must be the church on an inward journey before it can become the church on an outward journey.

As a Christian educator, I am convinced that the free evangelical tradition of the Christian church would have a radically different presence today had evangelism been associated appropriately with Christian social ministries. Had the curricular idea in Christian education been engaged by a synergistic process of social action and evangelism, the church would have a dramatically different appearance today.

Teaching

Teaching in the life of a church should be characterized by a dialogic base, a mission principle, and integrated movements.

A dialogic base recognizes and avoids the way persons hold and announce their beliefs monologically. Individuals may fail to see the possibilities of relationships between what they believe and the convictions of other persons. The responsibility of the role of teaching in the life of the local church is to engage in dialogue with each generation. Therein lies the seedbed for the renewal of the church. The Story is best understood when it is spoken in dialogue with the story of persons. The dialogic base requires these components. The teaching ministry of the church must engage us with an interior journey of the devotional life. We must be challenged with an exterior journey of witness and ministry. We must belong to the community in bonds of mutual accountability.

A mission principle accentuates the individual gifts for ministry and the resulting call to mission. In tandem, this principle emphasizes the corporate gifts and call to mission. A mission principle should permeate the organization of the local church. Deficiencies abound when a community is organized on a principle justified only because it is efficient or productive. We need an organizing principle that matches our vision. We need a mission principle that energizes and disciplines us. Gordon Cosby expressed the need like this:

A Christian structure exists to free people from their boundaries
and to provide healing for their wounds. The spirit infusing the
preparation for mission and informing the life in groups is all
important.[3]

The organization in which we teach is of the highest level of significance not only because it enhances our teaching, but because
the structure itself teaches. We must be concerned with the
lessons inherently communicated by the structures of the church.

Integrated movements call for the assimilation of various features into one harmonious expression. Teaching that is most
valued is purposeful. It is intentional. It is chosen after reflection.
It avoids the mindset that afflicts us when we say we are moving
from theory to practice in our teaching. Theory does not precede
practice. Practice and theory are twins. They each collapse into
the present moment. The best teaching theory in the church is
good practice. Conversely, the best teaching practice in the
church is good theory. Teaching should reflect a synergism.
Teaching is well-defined as the practice of the believing game and
the practice of the doubting game. In the doubting game we ask
the question, "What is wrong with this . . ." The believing game
calls for the commitment, "I am willing to entertain this . . ." For
the cherished moments in teaching and learning, I subscribe to
the insight, "Speech has a subservient role to choreography."

Christian teaching is illustrated by this helpful analogy. As
one drives the interstate systems of our nation, there are many
miles that cut through stone and rock formations. The mountain
ridge or hillside has been split open to provide a passage for the
interstate highway. In that cross section of the underground strata,
the bore holes are observable. A drill has been used, and detonation device inserted to create the passage. It was necessary to place
an explosive charge that would be of adequate power to open the
passage, but not so powerful that it would harm or destroy persons or property nearby. Teaching in faith growth requires an
explosive charge of adequate power, but not so powerful that it
would be destructive of persons. Such is the task of the teaching in
the life of the church. I believe the liberation theologians call it

dangerous memory. It is deceivingly simple to describe; it is devastatingly costly to embody.[4]

Groupings

Family

In the introductory pages of this book, I created a story about two families. In one example the woman who was traveling to work seemed to be disengaged with the environments surrounding her. Perhaps it was not disengagement so much as it was a denial of the needs of persons around her. Her family seemed to be unraveling in the exhaustion and stress that dominated her daily routines.

The needs of family provide a compelling argument for a reconceptualization of Christian education. Often we are guilty of pleading for families to spend more time together as a unit while planning family life programs sponsored by the church that are structured to separate families. We place children with children, youth with youth, and adults with adults!

In traditional structures of Christian education, we are led to the false conclusion that the prime response by the church to the needs of families is to bring them to church-sponsored events. Synergistic thinking will lead us to see the need to provide resources for utilization by families at times and places chosen by the family. Synergistic thinking will lead us to understand and accept more than stereotypical definitions of family (for example, single-parent families). Synergistic thinking will assist us in shaping support systems for families that create secure and challenging homes, welcome guests in biblical hospitality, encourage table culture by nurturing conversation, and move outside a home to neighbors in discipleship.

The church has a mission of hospitality. The home has a similar mission. Biblical images abound that support this idea. In Genesis 14, Abraham entertains angels by the oaks of Mamre. In Jesus' parable in Luke 14, a rich man invites the poor, the crippled, and the blind to his banquet.

Children

The record in Genesis reports that God felt a sense of delight in the created order. This sense of delight is that which surrounds creation. A child is blest if those who occupy the environment and relations of early childhood communicate messages of gladness and delight. The life of David in the Old Testament is a biblical model of development through stages. When Samuel anointed the young David, the story in 1 Samuel 16 tells us that a spirit of delight, of cosmic wonder was evident.[5]

Daniel Aleshire observes:

> The Christian community can learn from children, but it must also learn to examine some assumptions about the presence of children in congregational life. I do not think churches need more information about children nearly as much as they need to rethink the ways in which they deal with children.[6]

Even when they are disruptive, children have their place with the family of faith. Their attention spans are extremely limited. Aleshire continues, "If people don't intentionally develop attitudes of inclusion, they may practice exclusion by default."[7]

A Christian educator must proceed with sensitivity but also with tenacity in helping a congregation acknowledge prevailing attitudes toward children who are not socialized to the church environments. Disruptive or irreverent behavior must be analyzed for its causes.

It is also necessary to assist leaders in giving attention to children with special needs. The failure to be hospitable to special children is unintentional usually, but its perpetuation on that basis does not make it justifiable.

If the lessons of Matthew 25 are embodied in the synergism of Christian education, our faith communities will become leading advocates for children in our society. In Aleshire's opinion, "The churches . . . are at their best when they remember people who have been forgotten and seek to reconcile people who have been estranged."[8]

Youth

The biblical story of David also gives us an image of the adolescent. In 1 Samuel 17, David, the youth, arrives on the scene of battle playing the limited role assigned to someone of his tender years. To his amazement, his brothers and the army of the Hebrews are cowering before the taunts of Goliath.

One of the great things about the idealism of youth is that they show up with an attitude of possibility. They are not fatigued by problems in the manner of others. They throw themselves into the activity. Unjaded by life, David says—in John Claypool's paraphrase—"I will do what all the elders have concluded is impossible!"[9]

Like David, some youth accept the faith stories of their childhood and act on the assumption of the truthfulness in the story. Other youth are more apathetic or rebellious toward the story of the faith community. Daniel Aleshire comments, "The faith of youth is shaped and influenced by participation in the community of faith and by that community's expressions of ministry."[10]

Extremely important issues are involved when faith convictions interact with the curricular issues of discipleship for any person of any age. This is never more dramatically discovered than among persons of an adolescent age. As Aleshire puts it, "Adolescents are capable of spiritual genius."[11]

Our youth deserve our best witness to the whole gospel. When they are appropriately nurtured and prompted, their idealism can become a powerful force in the faithfulness of the church. A mature community can help youth construct a theological point of view that is biblically literate and theologically oriented. Once again, the synergy of faith growth calls for a connectedness, a pulsating vitality, an interactive movement.

Adults

In five decades, David rose from the obscurity of a shepherd boy to the status of the undisputed ruler between the Nile and Euphrates rivers. He had all kinds of natural instincts. He could do so many things well. Yet when he lived long enough to look back, life began to change. When he lived long enough to be the cause of pain and suffering on those he loved, life began to taste like ashes. Out of David's collision with reality and grief, however, he had a great experience of mercy. He found a new sense of identity because he discovered forgiveness and hope.[12]

The busyness of adults is a limiting factor in their faith growth. Many find that their careers have become increasingly stressful and filled with insecurities. Many adults, like David, have lived long enough to learn the response to the statement, "Life isn't fair." The response of the adult is, "Life is fair; we all suffer."

Some adults choose to live in a response of gratitude for what life offers. Other adults choose a response of entitlement for the benefits in their lives. Aleshire notes: "Either attitude will influence an individual's openness to grace, readiness to share, commitment to others, and a sense of responsibility."[13]

For the adult, faith growth happens in the synergy of the events of life and faith convictions. That synergy then reinterprets both faith and life. According to Aleshire, "The experiences of life influence the faith that adults fashion, and that faith redefines the experiences of life."[14]

Adults have the luxury and the curse of the accumulation of this synergy. Other developmental stages are so limited in the span of years and so preoccupied with the onward rush of events that reflection is difficult to engage. When adults are able to reflect, as one of the two women described in the introduction of this book, it is a luxury. When reflection is not experienced, as in the case of the other woman, it is impoverishing.

A Reflection on
Church Functions and Groupings

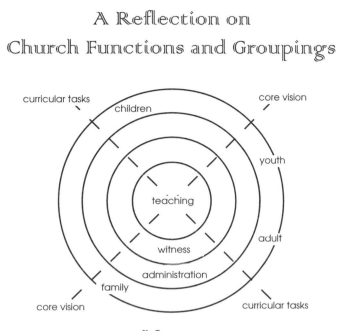

Notes

[1] Robert A. Raines, *Reshaping the Christian Life* (New York: Harper & Row, 1964) 70.

[2] Ibid., 73-74.

[3] Gordon Cosby, *Handbook for Mission Groups* (Waco TX: Word, 1975) 65.

[4] William B. Rogers, "Teaching in the Life of a Church," *Baptist History and Heritage*, XXVI (1991): 3-15.

[5] John Claypool, *Stages: The Art of Living the Expected* (Waco TX: Word, 1977) 21-33.

[6] Daniel O. Aleshire, *Faithcare: Ministering to All God's People Through the Ages of Life* (Philadelphia: Westminster, 1988) 95.

[7] Ibid.

[8] Ibid., 97.

[9] Claypool, 63-71.

[10] Aleshire, 139.

[11] Ibid., 141.

[12] Claypool, 63-71.

[13] Aleshire, 164.

[14] Ibid., 165.

Knowledge/News

In 1976, our family drove from our home in New Orleans, Louisiana, to southwestern Colorado for our first attempts at snow skiing. We made our way through the swamps of the Gulf Coast, across the plains of West Texas, and began the final five-hour road trip north of Albuquerque, New Mexico.

As we left the interstate system, we pushed on through the northwestern regions of New Mexico toward our destination, the San Juan mountains just north of Durango, Colorado. Even when compared with the swampland and the big sky of the plains, we found the barrenness of northwestern New Mexico to be extremely boring!

One year later, we returned to the ski area for the exhilaration we had discovered on the slopes of the Rocky Mountains. For this return trip, we were prepared. We decided we might make the dullness of the New Mexican landscape more bearable by reserving our most interesting books and magazines for that final five-hour segment. We purchased new 8-track tapes for that portion of our journey. In subsequent years, we even scheduled ourselves to make that five-hour trip after sunset since "there was nothing to see" in route.

By 1982, we were not only enjoying annual ski trips to southwestern Colorado, but we were learning to enjoy that wilderness area in other seasons of the year. In one of those summer experiences, our exploration of the area introduced us to the Chaco Culture National Historic Park, which contains numerous ruins of Indian villages that represent the highest point of prehistoric Pueblo civilization. In the summer of 1986, we devoted some of our visit to an introduction to the Anasazi, a native American people who inhabited that region from about 100 A.D. until their mysterious disappearance in the twelfth and thirteenth centuries. They are noted for their architectural construction of cliff dwellings, their artistic sophistication, and their curiosity related to astronomy.

Our perceptions of the barrenness and dullness associated with northwestern New Mexico were changing. Why? The knowledge we acquired made a difference. Our engagement with the prehistoric cultures that had moved across that same terrain began to awaken us. The knowledge of the first twelve centuries was having a bearing on our situation and our condition in the twentieth century. Static information was taking on vitality. Historical antecedents were beginning to interact with us in our car as we drove northwest out of Albuquerque.

The 1990 version of our trip out of Albuquerque demonstrates another example of knowledge becoming news. As I gathered reading material in a bookstore in Albuquerque, my eyes focused on a series of books with one titled *Roadside Geology of New Mexico*. As I scanned the book, I was startled to read this paragraph:

> The Sandia Mountains, which rise so boldly behind the city, are an east-tilted fault block of 1.4 billion-year-old Precambrian granite topped with 300 million-year-old Pennsylvania sedimentary rocks. The height of the mountains is emphasized by the subsidence of the Rio Grande Rift: Beneath the rift, the same sedimentary rocks are nearly 20,000 feet down. If we add to this figure the height of the mountains above Albuquerque—about 5,000 feet—we come up with total fault movement of 26,000 feet or about 5 miles![1]

For more than ten years, I had been driving into and out of Albuquerque, negotiating the roads over and alongside the Sandia Mountains and the Rio Grande River in a state that might best be described as "dumb and happy." Imagine the geologic event that the Rio Grande Rift reflects. The matching strata of rock that was aligned is now separated by five miles. The earth had moved in cosmic proportions! I had been awakened to my environment. I had acquired knowledge. The knowledge became breathtaking news. Never again will I visit Albuquerque in the attitude of boredom. Now I look at that landscape with awe and wonder.

The geologic and cultural news about northwestern New Mexico is uniquely available and relevant to the traveler making that geographic trip. Geologic and cultural news has had a bearing on my condition. I am a different traveler because of that news.

The trustworthiness of the books and guides conveying the news has had a bearing. National Park Service guides have brought the Pueblo and Anasazi people into my environment. Authors who have written of them from an anthropological perspective have taken me into their environment. Now I make the trip across the New Mexican landscape, and I am engaged with evidence of dramatic geologic history and stories of cultural history. What was barren and dull has become enchanting and enriching. Ignorance and prejudice have been supplanted by knowledge transformed into news. What was static information has become dynamic news. Now that five-hour trip has about it a pulse of life, an organic flow, a connectedness.

Locus of Authority

We do not engage in faith growth in a vacuum. Questions about the location of authority are encountered and reencountered over the span of years by both the individual and the community of faith. That encounter calls on the sources of external authority—the biblical and extrabiblical witnesses—and the source of the internal self—the inspiration of the spirit of God in communion with the believer. That encounter produces the synergism of the spiritually mature person.

Henri J. M. Nouwen tells this story of twins in the womb, talking to each other:

> The sister said to the brother, "I believe there is life after birth." Her brother protested vehemently, "No, no, this is all there is. This is a dark and cozy place, and we have nothing else to do but to cling to the cord that feeds us." The little girl insisted, "There must be something more than this dark place. There must be something else, a place with light where there is freedom to move." Still she could not convince her twin brother.

After some silence, the sister said hesitantly, "I have something else to say, and I'm afraid you won't believe that, either, but I think there is a mother." Her brother became furious. "A mother!" he shouted. "What are you talking about? I have never seen a mother, and neither have you. Who put that idea in your head? As I told you, this place is all we have. Why do you always want more? This is not such a bad place, after all. We have all we need, so let's be content."

The sister was quite overwhelmed by her brother's response and for a while didn't dare say anything more. But she couldn't let go of her thoughts, and since she had only her twin brother to speak to, she finally said, "Don't you feel these squeezes every once in a while? They're quite unpleasant and sometimes even painful." "Yes," he answered. "What's special about that?" "Well," the sister said, "I think that these squeezes are there to get us ready for another place, much more beautiful than this, where we will see our mother face to face. Don't you think that's exciting?"

The brother didn't answer. He was fed up with the foolish talk of his sister and felt that the best thing would be simply to ignore her and hope that she would leave him alone.[2]

In this story I see the interactive dialogue of synergy between the dynamic of the authority of the internal self and the authority of external sources. One twin voices the view of settled knowledge and consensus based on the experience of the moment. This appeals to the appetites of the realist and pragmatist in each of us. The other twin gives voice to the hope of transcendence and vitality of faith. This appeals to the appetite in each of us for idealism and theistic existentialism. In its entirety, the story contains knowledge based on multiple sources of authority that has the possibility of exploding into news.

There are many sources for authority and a variety of definitions given to modify the word authority. Do you know of persons and forces that possess power but lack genuine authority? Can you cite sources of political authority, historical authority, charismatic authority, and religious authority? External sources of authority may be found in education, but there are the limits of the mind. Authority may be found in politics, but there is the predictable clash of political forces. Often it is found in philosophy, but there are unintelligible answers and unsolvable problems. Authority may be lodged in science, but today's conclusions become tomorrow's processes. Internal sources of authority may be found in the capacity to believe, trust, respect, and worship. It may be found in unity, wholeness, and harmony (as in Shalom); but it is also located in irony, paradox, divergence, and the irrational.

If we surrender authority to the forces of our culture, then we will allow our culture to establish consensus, command assent, or preserve a particular ideology. In such an environment, faith growth will rest on what we feel and not be reflected in the synergy between what we feel *and* what we think. Faith growth will rest on majority opinion and not reflect the synergy of popular thought *and* prophetic insight.

If problem-solving is elevated to an authoritative process, then the theological concept of God as the unmoved Mover will be replaced by persons who become "the self-judging judger" and "the self-measuring measurer." In such a process we are condemned to conclude that authority cannot be found; it must be produced. Such a conclusion is spiritually destructive.

For Christian education, the will of God is the authoritative norm, and the life of Christ is the central revelation of that will. That divine will is sought in the inscrutable ways of God. We believe in what we appreciate, value, and savor—not in what we know in certitude and have the skills to control.

It is a mistake to think that we are without authority in the synergy of faith growth just because we do not prevail politically, or because we are rejected culturally, or because we have failed quantitatively.[3]

Liberating Discipline

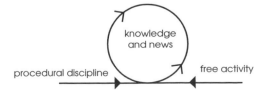

Let's think together about our lives and the dimensions we encounter or could encounter in our daily experiences. Life is composed of a certain number of hours and minutes out of each twenty-four hours consumed by the dictates of biological necessities. We must sleep and eat. There are days and nights when those two activities would be described as spontaneous and free. When we anticipate the aroma and savor the taste of our favorite food, there is a sense of exultation in a satisfying meal. The desired aromas and tastes on the palate do not occur spontaneously without careful preparation. Enjoying a delicious meal is an activity that depends on the synergism of procedural discipline and free activity (or in this illustration, a gourmet flair).

Another dimension of life common for all of us is described by two words: vocation and avocation. Vocation represents how we spend our time and energy for the purpose of gaining extrinsic rewards. We know that we need money at the survival level of our existence. Vocational compensation provides for the necessities of life and, to varying degrees, the luxuries of life. Some persons know their vocations as more than this, but some of us find the "more" in our avocations.

An avocation represents how we spend our time and energy for the purpose of gaining intrinsic rewards. We have discovered that physical exercise affects not only our bodies, but also our minds and emotions. A hobby changes the pace and rhythm of daily life in a rewarding manner. An avocation is pursued, in many instances, with the attitude, "I would pay someone to allow me the pleasure of this activity."

The skills developed in the workplace require procedural discipline. To the degree that the procedural discipline is mastered, the worker may move on to new assignments and rewards for productivity. Procedural discipline is also required in most hobbies and free activities, but the goal is not extrinsic but rather intrinsic rewards. A healthy approach to living will include both procedural discipline and free activity as expressed in the synergy of vocation and avocation.

In 1 Corinthians 8, Paul addresses the issue of liberating discipline:

Now concerning food sacrificed to idols: we know that "all of us possess knowledge." Knowledge puffs up, but love builds up. Anyone who claims to know something does not yet have the necessary knowledge; but anyone who loves God is known by him. . . .

But take care that this liberty of yours does not somehow become a stumbling block to the weak. For if others see you, who possess knowledge, eating in the temple of an idol, might they not, since their conscience is weak, be encouraged to the point of eating food sacrificed to idols? So by your knowledge those weak believers for whom Christ died are destroyed. But when you thus sin against members of your family, and wound their conscience when it is weak, you sin against Christ. Therefore, if food is a cause of their falling, I will never eat meat, so that I may not cause one of them to fall. (vv. 1-3, 9-13)

One central idea is that knowledge may have its benefits, but the violation of a loving attitude is not one of those benefits. True community exists among Christians when there is some healthy tension between free activity and disciplined procedure. When in any community, large or small, the members exercise their freedom to the neglect of their discipline, that community experiences chaos. When in any community the members exercise legalistic discipline to the neglect of personal freedom, a suffocating censorship sets in. For every freedom or right claimed from the community in which we worship, there is a corresponding discipline in or obligation to that community. What are the characteristics of this liberating discipline associated with faith growth?

There is the characteristic of a clear and unequivocal commitment to the weakest, poorest, and the most abused persons in our society. If I am a parent, I will nurture in my children informed hearts and minds toward those who "live on the margins." If I am a Christian educator, I will work with teachers and leaders to inform their visions of the Christ who wipes away our own tears, and the Christ who waits outside at the wailing walls of "those who are not like us." I will attempt to nurture our community to build into our lives structures of accountability and structures of liberation.[4]

There is the commitment to dialogic principles throughout the congregation and its relationships. More cautious members of groups will need to resist the tendency to reduce all the risk in plans for the future. More fearless members will need to resist the habit of forging ahead in self-righteousness. According to Elizabeth O'Connor, when important issues need attention, both types of members must learn to conduct the dialogue

> within the context of a passionate waiting on God. . . . We do not enter into dialogue in order to persuade another to see things our way. . . . We are open to change and are aware that our lives need correcting. . . . Dialogue requires a clear, radical, and arduous commitment to listening.[5]

This liberating synergy requires that we learn new ways of living together as God's people. Most of us have not faced a disciplined way of receiving the information that others have about us, that we do not have about ourselves. This receptivity is not only a problem for individuals; more radically, it is a problem for groups in congregations. John P. Diggins comments,

> Groups must be critical contemplatives of their corporate lives. This is one way of protecting the dissenter, the one who sometimes turns out to be the prophet, and is too often ignored or stoned. . . . Groups are even slower than individuals to change, admit mistakes, or embody humility.[6]

To reflect critically on one's own life and the life of one's faith community is to enable the synergistic interplay of knowledge and news. Can you supply illustrations of groups in churches admitting or embodying humility? Faith growth demands this characteristic in the church.

Finally, the characteristic of liberating discipline is the commitment to a life of reflection. This quality refers to gaining an objective perspective on our work, understanding how our behavior is viewed by others, and attempting to understand how the mind of Christ might see our activities and sponsored values. In reflection, the emotional and the intellectual come into a synergism. In reflection, we pause in the midst of study or ministry or community or worship and ask such questions as:

What do we see ourselves doing?
What do we hear ourselves cherishing?
What are we willing to give up?
What do we feel we should hold on to?

We are searching for liberating discipline. We are hoping and praying for knowledge that blossoms into news.

Learning from Experience

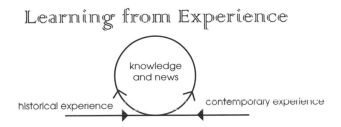

What kind of religious music do you prefer? My hunch is that you have an immediate answer to this question. My prediction is that within the broad ranges of styles and types of religious music, you have rather informed preferences for performers and artists who are identified with more specific styles and types. Your answer will not require research and thought over a period of hours. Your answer will be immediate and direct.

Christian educators have rarely understood and implemented the power of religious music in the movements of Christian education. Specifically, I believe that faith growth should recognize the medium of music to synergize the historical experience and the contemporary experience. Religious music that nurtures the soul is evidence of a balance between that which is valued from the past and that which is valued in the present. What better example could there be than religious music as a vehicle to nurture knowledge into news? What better example than religious music as capable of generating an atmosphere in which the historical and the contemporary find a connectedness? What better example than religious music to become a powerful river that expresses "O God, Our Help in Ages Past" and "Just a Closer Walk with Thee"?

We can expend enormous energy and time debating theological creeds and denominational statements of faith. If those creeds and statements could be set to appealing musical frames, I doubt the same debates would consume us. On one hand, we should recognize that religious music can convey inaccurate, even heretical ideas. It can convey a kind of theological laziness. On the other hand, religious music also encourages us to be more ecumenical and less provincial. The poets and musicians who provide our religious music are not examined with the prejudices that restrict our selection of other sources in Christian education.

How has the music of the church played a role in your faith growth? How could we as Christian educators employ the music of the church more intentionally in the teaching ministry of the church? How could we acknowledge the energy of religious music to focus historical experience and contemporary experience?

Things can be experienced in the contemporary environment yet not be understood. Current experience and the value assigned to it can lead to the conviction that problem-solving methods are all we need. We can experience the solution to almost everything and still come away knowing nothing. The historical experience assigns values to being and to knowing. The contemporary experience assigns value to doing and to acting. There are those who try to convince us that contemporary experiences are all we need because they give us the means of testing in experimental procedures. Others remind us of the evaluative standards in historical ideas and related experiences.[7]

In 1985, at Southern Baptist Theological Seminary in Louisville, Kentucky, we decided to plan a festival for October 1986 to celebrate the teaching ministry of Findley Edge. The planning group wanted to honor Dr. Edge for significant contributions in Christian education. He had led us to see the historical significance of the role of the laity, *and* he had been immersed in the contemporary movements of lay renewal. The teaching ministry of the church had been expressed in his published writing in both its historical and biblical concepts and in the contemporary application of teaching methods. Dr. Edge had insisted that Christian education could not be pursued historically in a vacuum. It could not be practiced contemporaneously without sensitivity to its root systems.

Two objectives dominated our planning. The Edge Festival should be attractive to those practicing the ministry of Christian education. It also should be faithful to those contributions of Findley Edge listed in the previous paragraph. We faced the questions: How could the festival happen in the restrictions of time, space, and other resources? How could its theme be preserved into the future?

We found at least one answer to our questions. I went to my colleague and friend, Milburn Price, and asked that he agree to write both a text and music for the occasion. Over a period of a year, the two of us talked about Dr. Edge's contributions. Dr. Price asked me to delineate three themes that had been prominent in Dr. Edge's work. I gave him this list:

- the importance of continuing pilgrimage toward mature faith
- the diversity of tasks of ministry to which persons are called
- the inclusiveness of the call to ministry, embracing male and female, clergy and laity, and persons of varying theological perspectives.

Using the gifts with which he is endowed, Dr. Price produced a hymn that was first sung in the seminary chapel on October 27, 1986. Today that hymn, "Believers All, We Bear the Name," is published in several hymnals.

The knowledge of the historical experience and the knowledge of the contemporary experience were fashioned into a synergy. That knowledge blooms and flowers now through the medium of music. As I write these words nine years later, the sensations of the lectures and workshops of the festival have faded. The memory of the celebrations have lost some clarity. But the music and its passion and reason can be and has been encountered as the contemporary experience and the historical experience have floated into the synergistic possibility of knowledge becoming news in Christian education. Through music, that tune and text, in their vitality, are as available today as they were in 1986.

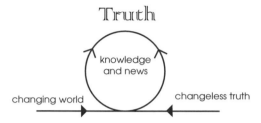

Regrettably, we live in a world in which the search for truth is hampered by the fact that we can gain knowledge without gaining truth. We can hold power without authority. We can pursue an existence without purpose. We can possess information about history without the meaning of history possessing us. In that world in our better moments, we acknowledge these yearning desires:

Help me to know!
Help me to see!
Help me to feel!
Help me to hear!
Show me the truth!

Should Christian education be approached with the understanding that the truth is a pyramid to be filled with more correct information?

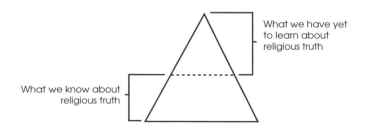

Should Christian education be approached with the understanding that some portion of the truth in the pyramid will never be known to us in this world?

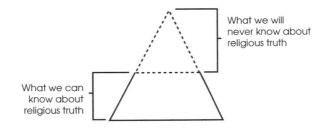

Should Christian education be approached with the understanding that what we know as truth serves primarily to give us a place to stand and witness the expanding, mysterious qualities of truth?

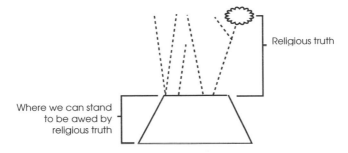

Should Christian education be approached in a radically different fashion? Would we have a more mature and informed view if we avoided the pyramid image and thought in terms of a synergistic image composed of circular lines and interactive arrows that show connectedness?

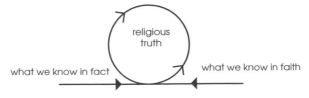

We Christian educators live in a world of religious rhetoric searching for truth within the language that surrounds us. Some use religious rhetoric to expand personal freedom, while others use it to diminish personal freedom. There are those who use religious arguments to respect the consciences of those whose beliefs differ from their own. Others use religious arguments to be suspicious of the consciences of those whose beliefs differ from their own.

There are Christian educators who have subscribed to the statement that the one we name God is larger than our understanding. Others seem to have subscribed to the statement that the one God we name is circumscribed by our understanding. Religious leaders use religious language to admit limited knowledge of the motives of others. Other religious leaders claim omniscient knowledge of the motives of others.

Some leaders in religion are committed to engaging the cognitive dimensions of human decision-making. Others are skilled at bypassing the cognitive dimensions of human decision-making. Some religious groups enjoy the search for truth in the company of other seekers. Others sit in judgment on those who do not have the truth in the identical vocabulary.

There are religious leaders who promote the medicine of mercy rather than the medicine of hatred. Some religious communities have made a commitment to inclusiveness, while others seem to be devoted to strategies of exclusiveness. There are religious organizations that have adopted the governing idea that majority rule does not grant a license for majority tyranny, while others seem to have adopted the governing idea that 51 percent of the voters should get 100 percent of the power.

Events among religious groups have demonstrated that there are those who blindly stumble into slavery, while others refuse to enter into slavery voluntarily. Between these polarities of religious values and religious rhetoric, there can be no synergy of the knowledge and news of truth.[8]

A Reflection on Knowledge and News

I have concluded this section on the knowledge and news of faith growth for those readers who respond to theoretical ideas as well as other readers who are responsive to practical strategies. The following is a list of synergistic questions for the Christian educator to consider:

• How well are my daily and weekly functions reflecting my faith convictions?
• How accurately do I demonstrate fidelity to the movements in educational ministry I claim to follow?
• Am I utilizing the best tools available to me in assessing the needs of persons and groupings? When did I last incorporate a new tool of assessment?
• Which trends do I ignore for good reason? Which trends must I acknowledge? How?
• How many different strategies/programs/resources for corporate and private Bible study are we facilitating as a congregation for each of the four groupings? How recently did we add or delete? Why?
• How many different strategies/programs/resources for corporate and private discipleship are we making available as a congregation for each of the four groupings? How recently did we add or delete? Why?
• How many different strategies/programs/resources for encouraging and enriching community are we enabling as a congregation for each of the four groupings? How recently did we add or delete? Why?
• How many different strategies/programs/resources for corporate and private worship are we coordinating as a congregation for each of the four groupings? How recently did we add or delete? Why?

A Reflection on Faith Growth

This vision statement for faith growth in Christian education has been written out of the conviction that there are those of us who have the assignment to wander in the wilderness of thoughts about religious nurture, where there are a limited number of sure land-marks and not enough experienced guides. Our task is to put up a few signs and leave markers to allow those who follow to walk into the land that has been shown to us. We simply have the task of witnessing to our children and other scattered pilgrims that the paradigm shifts and the third waves and the synergisms in that land are not as giants, but that it indeed is a land flowing with milk and honey.

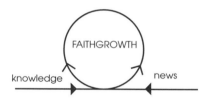

Notes

[1]Halka Chronic, *Roadside Geology of New Mexico* (Missoula MT: Mountain Press, 1987) 98.

[2]Henri Nouwen, *Our Greatest Gift* (San Francisco: Harper Collins, 1994) 19, 20.

[3]John P. Diggins, *The Promise of Pragmatism* (Chicago: University of Chicago Press, 1994). For a number of years I have been persuaded that pragmatism offers a false promise to Christian education. Throughout this chapter, evidence may be found that I am informed by this synergis-tic work of Professor Diggins. This book has enabled me to find a voice.

[4]Elizabeth O'Connor, *The New Community* (New York: Harper & Row, 1976) 100.

[5]Ibid., 103.

[6]Ibid., 105.

[7]Diggins.

[8]Ibid.